Published by People's Press

Post Office Box 70
Woody Creek, Colorado 81656
www.PeoplesPress.org

People's Press Mission
*As the world becomes increasingly global, the need grows for
community and for the cultivation of community identity
through artistic insight. People's Press will search for books
and the means to publish and distribute them to this purpose.*

People's Press editorial board
Mirte Mallory
Nicole Beinstein Strait
George Stranahan

Library of Congress Control Number: 2012954909
ISBN: 978-1-936905-99-7

Written by George Stranahan
Photographs by George Stranahan
Book design by Rainy Day Designs

Typeset in ITC Stone Serif and Univers
Printed in Canada

A Predicament of Innocents

Might the schools help?

People's Press

"Is 4 the 4 for everybody?
Are all sevens equal?
When the convict ponders the light is
it the same light that shines on you?"

—Pablo Neruda

INTRODUCTION

A gaggle of geese; a pride of lions; a predicament of innocents.

Predicament, *n.* 1. An unpleasant, difficult, perplexing, or dangerous situation.

Innocent, *adj.* 1.Free from moral wrong, not involving evil intent or motive. Having or showing the simplicity or naiveté of an unworldly person, guileless, ingenuous, uninformed or unaware, ignorant. A young child.

> *"The moral universe rests upon the*
> *breath of schoolchildren."*
>
> —Rabbi Yehuda Nisiah, CE 250

What we do about all of this is to confine them to school. Schools are certainly not the result of intelligent design, and certainly a consequence of continual evolution. Looked back upon, evolution is always boring: survival of the fittest, never the underdog. There are many, many interacting parts to the educational system, and they each evolve according to their institutional self-interests. The current edition makes growing up a matter of receiving huge amounts of instruction in academics, followed by extensive testing on the subject matter. Just like us in our time, children today forget it soon after the final exam. The education system has evolved, unguided, in the most unimaginative way possible: to make the kids grow up to be just like us.

"Education" is a word we hear regularly, and the word shloshed about in that muddle we call "mind" will conjure up images, memories, emotions, connections, and probably other concepts we haven't even learned to name yet.

They're not going to be the same for you as they are for me. I remember the shameless surprise I felt when my third-grade teacher sent me to the principal's office for responding to her question by jumping onto the desk and yelling, "Me no know, and me no care." I can still smell the first time I finger-painted, and see again that blue swirl that my palm created. Often the word "education" brings up an image of a building, some generic multistory brick structure with regular rows of windows announcing the regularities of the classrooms within. Sometimes the image is a hallway—not generic, but, for me, that hallway I walked down in elementary school to get to the bathroom.

You, of course, have constructed your own understanding of the word "education," and yet we understand each other without going into hours of storytelling. We, perhaps more than children themselves, recognize childhood as a special estate, fragile enough that society feels obligated to discover and provide special supports that we name "education." Society designs, redesigns, and then redesigns again its systems to educate children; the word comes from the Latin *educare*, "to lead them out," in this case of their childhood.

"At the heart of the educational process lies the child. Children need to be themselves, to live with other children and grownups, to learn from their environment, to enjoy the present, to get ready for the future, to create and to love, to learn to face adversity, to behave responsibly, in a word, to be human beings."

—The Plowden Report (1967)
OF THE CENTRAL ADVISORY COUNCIL FOR EDUCATION, ENGLAND

The math teacher was delivering instruction to an eighth-grade class on the Common Core State Standards of bivariate probability distributions, and a kid asked, "Do I need to know this?" The teacher answered, "You need it to graduate." The kid did not ask the logical next question: "Do I need to graduate?"

So the purpose of the teaching and learning of bivariate probabilities is to graduate, and if we then ask, "What is the purpose of graduating?" we hear a great empty sigh followed by, "Duh, let's see, to get a job, right? Or to go to college?" I suppose after that we might ask, "What is the purpose of going to college?" And the answer: "Duh, to get a better job." A job that requires no knowledge whatsoever of bivariate probability distributions.

Because we don't have an ongoing dialogue on the purpose of education, we fall back to the amoral default "To get a job." One reason that we fail to have the dialogue is because it would surely be political, and we customarily deny that education could be about politics, politics as morality, the differences we describe as between left and right, soft and hard, dove and hawk.

"Politics, a weighing of dreams against fears, is a civilization's dialogue with itself." This phrase from a front-page article in the *Wall Street Journal* sticks with me.

I daresay we are afraid to have the debate. We are divided, so close to equally, among a morality of dreams: soft, dove, collaboration, liberal on one side, and fears, hard, hawk, competition, conservative on the other. Neither side wishes to force the dialogue for fear of losing, losing something they value very highly for their own children. The only acceptable middle ground for the dialogue on education defaults to the amoral one: It's about jobs. Once we settle the debate here at "jobs," we are left to argue over the relatively less-divisive issues of standards and assessments. And so we have an eighth-grade math standard on bivariate distributions that, I daresay, has nothing to do with either politics or jobs. Is that standard there because we failed to have the dialogue?

There are other areas where we avoid the moral showdown, the role of government beyond public education among them. One side says big and maybe more, the other says small and certainly less. We don't settle down and hash out what is *good* government, what's the *right* size in order to have good government. You see, the opposing moralities have entirely different views of good education and good government. As long as we duck these dialogues, the establishments of the status quo that suck the blood out of these institutions are safe and profitable. We have governance of schools and nations according to the politics described by Ambrose Bierce: "Politics [is a] strife of interests masquerading as a contest of principles." We indeed go out of our way to avoid that contest of principles.

James Madison, in his Federalist Paper dated November 23, 1787, writes, "By a faction, I understand a number of citizens, whether amounting to a majority or a minority of the whole, who are united and actuated by some common impulse of passion, or of interest, adversed to the rights of other citizens, or to the permanent and aggregate interests of the community."

Richard Elmore writes in *School Reform from the Inside Out*,

> There is, of course, strong evidence that asking policymakers (elected representatives) to bring coherence and stability to education policy at the state and local level is akin to trying to change the laws of gravity. Instability and incoherence in the form of pluralist politics are the rule; coherence and stability, the exception. Pluralism—organized factions mobilizing and using political institutions as a means for legitimizing their particular interests in public policy—is hardwired into the culture and institutional structure of American politics. James Madison, in Federalist #10, puts the matter succinctly: institutions of government exist to play the interests of competing factions against each other, so as to prevent the tyranny of one faction over all others.

We are doomed by our devotion to our many factions, legitimate or not, to avoid the tyranny that would result from resolving the conflict of principles. In a pure democracy the majority could vote a knockout blow to a minority; in a republic we have all these institutions and establishments to protect against such a blow.

Madison again: "The influence of factious leaders may kindle a flame within their particular States, but will be unable to spread a general conflagration through the other States."

OK, so we don't get a national agreement for the purposes of education based on moral principles, either progressive or conservative. I'm ready to settle for "It's about jobs in a society committed to environmental and economic justice." Here, I am afraid we will simply uncover the great moral divide between a liberal and a conservative understanding of justice.

> *"In too many cases, people fight their political*
> *and cultural wars on children's playgrounds.*
> *As in all wars, the first casualty is truth,*
> *the second casualty is children."*
>
> —Philip Uri Treisman

> *"We live, after all, in dark times, times with little historical mem-*
> *ory of any kind. There are vast dislocations in industrial towns,*
> *erosions of trade unions; there is little sign of class consciousness*
> *today. Our great cities are burnished on the surfaces, building high*
> *technologies, displaying astonishing consumer goods. And on the*
> *side streets, in the crevices, in the burnt-out neighborhoods, there*
> *are the rootless, the dependent, the sick, the permanently unem-*
> *ployed. There is little sense of agency, even among the brightly*
> *successful; there is little capacity to look at things as if they could*
> *be otherwise … These are dark and shadowed times, and we need*
> *to live them, standing before one another, open to the world."*
>
> —Maxine Greene

Think of public education as a large public works project, like highways, canals, the military, etc.

There is a need to contract out many pieces of any big project to private industry. Of course, there are the usual democratic rules, that any and all civilian companies are free and equal in competition to bid on all or parts of the project. The awarding of contracts, however, largely becomes a matter of cronyism, nepotism, political back-scratching, and even outright corruption. Let's follow the money: direct spending for public education is around $550 billion, of which about $10 billion is federal—not counting this past couple of years of stimulus spending. The remainder is split about fifty-fifty between state funding (fifty states) and local property-tax funding (15,000 school districts). This is extremely decentralized command and control of spending on public education!

Needless to say, there are countless organizations, committees, councils, philan-thropies, think tanks, university departments, etc. attracted to this many public teats. None of their revenue (originating from foundations and special interests) and spend-ing is accounted for in the $550 billion. Most of the funders, government agencies large and small, are ill-equipped to be discriminating or demanding in their con-tract negotiations. There's all the stuff bought for classrooms and schools: textbooks, electronics, whiteboards, tests, test scoring, supplements for everything, toilet paper, and guess what? The school janitor doesn't pick the toilet bowl cleanser; the district contracts for it. The school board has no idea how to do its job, and so contracts for all sorts of advice and training. The board assumes that its teachers and administrators don't know how to do their jobs either, and contracts for all sorts of advice and training for them. Hence all the associations and think tanks do all this advising and consulting and making recommendations to policymakers on the policies necessary to improve an education system that neither they nor the policymakers understand at all. And so they contract to produce and sell to school boards a study on toilet bowl cleansers …

I have constructed a visual metaphor for this system; at its core there is the big piece of meat that is the schools, administrators, teachers, students, janitors, and bus drivers that are, well, the meat of the educational system. The meat is covered with blowflies, outside contractors and advisors (such as the Bible Literacy Project, National School Safety and Security Services, American Reading Company, the Blue Bird bus company, the Center for Research on Education Outcomes, and on and on) whose survival depends upon living off the meat. Together they are more than enough to cover every bit of exposed meat. Should any portion of the meat be left exposed, there would be five flies buzzing around to lay their eggs. The end result is that the meat is entirely covered by blowflies. We, the public, see none of the meat, only the blowflies.

Naturally, the blowflies are interested in either preserving the status quo or expanding their portion of the meat. Fundamentally, their self-interest is not served by having the meat change in any way. So hold that image in your mind of the meat covered completely by blowflies that are determined to resist change, and understand why our education system is, and has been, so resistant to change. The meat is locked in the embrace of its blowflies, and the blowflies have locked arms to this purpose. To look at our public education system is to see blowflies.

> *"Precisely because education should be the lever for*
> *social transformation, it cannot be! … He or she knows*
> *that education is not the lever for the revolutionary*
> *transformation precisely because it should be! This*
> *contradiction is at the heart of the problem. In order*
> *for education to be the tool for transformation it would*
> *be necessary for the ruling class in power to commit*
> *suicide. It would have to give up its dominant*
> *power in society, including its creation and*
> *supervision of the schools and colleges."*
>
> —Paulo Freire

"Local control"—I call it Horace Mann's compromise. In exchange for the state-by-state adoption of compulsory schooling, the states were promised the freedom to do it any way they saw fit. State by state this freedom was passed down to local education agencies, a.k.a. school districts, now some 15,000 total in the United States, and generally governed by elected school boards. Almost universally school board members are not educators, but rather politically conservative and righteous laypeople who run on platforms built on maintaining the status quo and knowing for damn sure "right" from "wrong." It is quite common to find a school board candidate running on the basis of his or her business experience alone.

There is the true core of a school, the classroom and its teacher, curriculum, lesson plans, record keeping, assessment, discipline, and the multiple interpersonal complexities of teachers' and students' lives in the classroom. Then there is the administration; someone, after all, must make the rules.

"Administration in education means not the management of instruction but the management of structures and processes around instruction. That which cannot be managed must be protected from external scrutiny. Buffering consists of creating structures and procedures around the technical core of teaching that at the same time, 1) protect teachers from outside intrusions in their highly uncertain and murky work, and 2) create the appearance of rational management of the technical core, so as to allay the uncertainties of the public about the actual quality or legitimacy of what is happening in the technical core. This buffering creates what institutional theorists call a 'logic of confidence' between public schools and their constituents."

—Richard Elmore

What we ask teachers to do and what they do are not the same thing. The system will try to hide that fact from you. There will be conflict if we pry too much. If we knew what teachers really do, we'd probably approve, but there's just no time or place to talk about that. Philip Jackson calls teachers "gladiators of ambiguity."

In other words, "local control" has essentially no effect on the education of children. Maybe it's just as well that nonprofessionals, the board and its administrators, confine themselves to maintaining public confidence and leave the classroom to the teachers—as long as *someone* is establishing some standards. Colorado is typical in its constitution (1876) with Article 5, Section 25 that reads, "The General Assembly shall not pass local or special laws ... providing for the management of common schools." Would that be because the federal government has taken care of this? No, the United States Constitution mentions education in no article or amendment, while Amendment 10 reads, "The powers not delegated to the United States by the Constitution, nor prohibited by it to the States, are reserved to the States respectively, or to the people." This recipe, the feds are hands-off, the states are hands-off, and school districts ineffective, results in the public education system that we have. No system as large, bureaucratic, and hierarchical as public education will leave control and decision-making in the hands of the bottommost level, the classroom. Such a system reflexively and in self-interest will devise unbidden systems that allow them to truly declare, "Don't worry, everything is under control."

George Bush signed the No Child Left Behind Act (NCLB) of 2002, which required states to write standards, to test students relative to their standards, and to "fix" schools unable to pass the standards, without telling them what standards to use or what tests to give. Colorado, along with all other states, adopted standards and, in its case, designed the hated Colorado Student Assessment Program (CSAP). Very few would say that NCLB has substantially improved public education, but it did establish that the federal government could and would pass legislation in the education arena as a matter of civil rights while in no way threatening the principle of local control. If the disadvantaged achieve test scores equal to the advantaged, then we can declare the achievement of social justice, reduced simply to presumed equal opportunity, to be defined in this utterly trivial and unjust manner.

"Perhaps the greatest idea that America has
given the world is the idea of education for all.
The world is entitled to know whether this idea
means that everybody can be educated,
or only that everybody must go to school."

—Robert Hutchins

"Healthy nations have healthy schools, it's not the other way around." John I. Goodlad said that. Since there are no easy answers or simple solutions, I take this to be a simple description of our national predicament. Who can believe that if we eliminate the "achievement gap," the difference in test scores between the rich and the poor, that we have fixed the nation? I worry that if the scores should equalize by some cause or other, the nation would exclaim, "We've won the war on poverty! The poor now have equal educational opportunity, and that's all America is required to do about poverty." We could pick up our marbles and go home.

A new book by Theresa Perry, Robert Moses, Joan Wynne, Ernesto Cortés Jr., and Lisa Delpit, *Quality Education as a Constitutional Right*, argues for a constitutional amendment guaranteeing every citizen a quality education. This would place the word "education" in the Constitution and allow federal intervention into what states once considered to be theirs alone. Of course I believe it's one's right to get a quality education, and not just a right, but a necessity for the general good of mankind if there is to be any chance of achieving justice for all. The amendment would allow the federal government to drive the dialogue about what is a quality education and how the schools should be held accountable for its delivery. I know already how many arguments I have had at the local level about what constitutes a quality educational experience; there is deep disagreement between conservatives and liberals. But until we pass this kind of amendment, we can avoid a national argument. If we do pass the amendment, there will surely be lawsuits that end up in the Supreme Court; will they do a better job than my local school district at defining, let alone guaranteeing the delivery of, a quality education?

I wonder if the argument would be simpler if the proposed amendment guaranteed every citizen a healthy school—"healthy" meaning "without disease"—and we could talk about prevention rather than remediation. Having the discussion won't make us a healthy nation, but it's undoubtedly necessary in order to have a healthy nation.

> *"If the schools of a democratic society do not exist for and work for the support and extension of democracy, then they are either socially useless or socially dangerous. At the best they will educate people who will go their way and earn their living indifferent to the obligations of citizenship in particular and of the democratic way of life in general … But quite likely they will educate people to be enemies of democracy—people who will fall prey to demagogues, and who back movements and rally round leaders hostile to the democratic way of life. Such schools are either futile or subversive. They have no legitimate reason for existence."*
>
> —JAMES MURSELL

As we know, there is now a strong effort to create a set of national "standards" to specify what education is supposed produce, at least in the arena of knowledge and skills.

The effort shows surprising support: forty-eight states have adopted the Common Core State Standards, or standards similar to them.[1] If all the states voluntarily adopt the same set of standards, they will clearly be national, though not federally mandated.

Debbie Meier is an educator; it's what she does and has done with her adult life. She began teaching elementary school in Chicago, moved to Philly, and when she moved to NYC became involved with education at City College. In 1974 District 4 Superintendent Tony Alvarado picked her to become the founding teacher of an open classroom school, Central Park East in East Harlem. Meier, author of the inspiring book *The Power of Their Ideas*,[2] argues that:

> I'm for "standards" if we are talking about a flag held high to see where we are going. But as a euphemism for a K–12 curriculum, standards are a bad idea. Setting fixed standards for what students should learn means aiming either too low or too high—never on target for each individual learner.

> Before we decide which methods work in moving learners forward, we have to at least discuss "to what ends?" Effective standards—of any kind— uphold both our purposes and our good taste. People quite reasonably disagree on purposes. Some people may be willing to sacrifice a lot for Purpose A but very little for Purpose B. A group may agree on 10 goals for a good writing course, for instance, but disagree if forced to cut back to five. And good taste? Many books eventually declared classics were at first turned down by publishers and slammed by critics.

> Every time we try to fix goals for public schooling, we end up in the same fix as the constitutional originalists (who assume the U.S. Constitution has one immutable meaning); we sacrifice flexibility for immutability.

1. See www.corestandards.org.
2. In this book, written in 1994, Meier recounts a very pleasant history of Central Park East. Her email is deborah.meier@gmail.com.

It's a fact that we don't know how to teach math well to everyone. Maybe we never will. It might be fruitful to question the assumption that "everyone" must know advanced algebra (as opposed to, say, advanced musicianship). We should also ask what it will cost those who never "get" algebra—or some other core subject—if the trend continues to make mastering algebra a roadblock to further study. Why don't we remove the roadblock instead?

The one demand I'd like to make of U.S. schools is that they give young people the tools to lead a powerful public life: to be knowledgeable and thoughtful about democracy and the U.S. Constitution. After that, let's provide choices where we can without polarizing the democracy we are trying to nourish.

Meier is currently a senior scholar and adjunct professor at New York University's Steinhardt School of Culture, Education, and Human Development. She has founded public schools serving low-income minority students in New York City and Boston.

I know and understand that the public has an interest in and a right to ask, "Just what are you *doing* to our kids with our money?" I'm sorry that the education establishment responded with, and the public accepts, a set of Common Core Standards. Teachers would say, "There's so very much more." At Central Park East the standards are simply to work continually on developing the child's habits of the mind. These are their essential questions underlying all essential questions:

- From whose viewpoint are we seeing or hearing or reading? From what angle or perspective?
- How do we know what we know? What's the evidence and how reliable is it?
- How are things, events, or people connected to each other? What is the cause and what is the effect? How do they "fit" together?

- What if …? Could things be otherwise? What are or were the alternatives? Supposing.
- So what? What does it matter? What does it all mean? Who cares?

"For us education signifies an initiation into new ways of seeing, hearing, feeling, moving. It signifies a special kind of reflectiveness and expressiveness, a reaching out for meanings, a learning to learn."

—Maxine Greene

"A wise man will not go out of his way for information," Henry David Thoreau said circa 1850. Was he that much ahead of his time, some 150 years before what is now called the information age? No, I can't believe that he was foreseeing radio, TV, and the Internet; he was speaking to his own age, and his words happen to be timeless. There is information appropriate to and necessary for a man's way, and there is information superfluous to a man's way. It is the latter to which Thoreau speaks. I've been thinking about this as I watch our nation put forth Common Core Standards, what students should know and be able to do at various class levels. What I hear Thoreau saying that has meaning for today is that these standards need to be held to the standard that they are not superfluous to our individual and collective ways.

Well, there are a lot of ways in life, including the way of the child. The phrase "Common Core Standards" implies that these standards are not about all possible ways, but perhaps about some essential elements common to all possible ways. I have studied these 2010 standards in English and mathematics and declare them to be no more than just the way to get into college. The unexamined American assumption is that college is the grand boulevard of all good ways, and that spending thirteen years getting there is thus a way in itself.

I found the 1990 report "Reshaping School Mathematics" by the National Research Council to be closer to a way:

> To the Romans a *curriculum* was a rutted course that guided the path of two-wheeled chariots. Today's mathematics curriculum follows a deeply rutted path directed more by events of the past than by the changing needs of the present. Vast numbers of specific learning objectives, each with associated pedagogical strategies, serve as mileposts along the trail mapped by texts from kindergarten until twelfth grade. Problems are solved not by observing and responding to the natural landscape through which the mathematics curriculum passes, but by mastering time-tested routines conveniently placed along the path near every anticipated problem. Students who progress through this curriculum develop a kind of mathematical myopia in which the goal is to solve artificial word problems rather than realistic world problems.

> Few have the stamina to survive the curriculum of mathematics—at least not the way it is now delivered. Of 4 million who begin, only 500,000 are still studying mathematics 12 years later. Most students receive little of lasting value (*beyond acceptance into a college*) from the final mathematics course they study—typically high school geometry or Algebra II. Many of those who drop out harbor life-long feelings of guilt or distaste for school mathematics. Some of those who become disenchanted with mathematics become teachers; others help to decide educational and research policy for the nation.

The idea that the mathematical preparations required for entrance to college are equal to education is as ridiculous as the idea that mowing a lawn is equal to gardening.

> The changes in mathematics needed for intelligent citizenship have been significant. Most obvious, perhaps, is the need to understand data presented in a variety of different formats: percentages, graphs, charts,

tables, and statistical analyses are commonly used to influence societal decisions ... Citizens who cannot interpret quantitative data are, in this day and age, functionally illiterate.

A confused public often resorts to some form of media punditry, and media pundits know well that the public does not want to hear that "The issue is very complicated and there are no easy answers."

To realize a new vision of school mathematics will require public acceptance of a realistic philosophy of mathematics that reflects both mathematical practice and pedagogical experience. One cannot properly constitute a framework for a mathematics curriculum unless one first addresses two fundamental questions:

- What is mathematics?
- What does it mean to know mathematics?

Although few mathematicians or teachers spend much time thinking about these philosophical questions, the unstated answers that are embedded in public and professional opinion are the invisible hands that control mathematics education. Unless the guidance system for mathematics education is permanently reset to new and more appropriate goals, it will surely steer the curriculum back to its old path after every innovation.

Indeed, public education can change only when the public changes. We have lost our way until we do this.

"School, finally, isn't about disciplines and subjects,
but about what they were originally meant to do—
help the young make more sense of life, more sense of
experience, more sense of an unknowable future."

—MARION BRADY

A Predicament of Innocents

J ohn Franklin Bobbitt worried about effiency in education: teach what is necessary and eliminate the unnecessary.

In his 1915 book *What the Schools Teach and Might Teach* he observes, "Since schools are to fit people for social conditions, and since these conditions are continually changing, the work of the schools must correspondingly change." Bobbitt also thought that the curriculum has to adapt to the needs of individuals in their future roles in society; people should not be taught what they would never use. He influenced the curriculum by showing how teaching classical subjects should be replaced by teaching subjects that correspond to social needs. "Educate the individual according to his capabilities. This requires that the material of the curriculum be sufficiently various to meet the needs of every class of individuals in the community and that the course of training and study be sufficiently flexible that the individual can be given just the things that he needs."

Bobbitt is describing what we now label as "tracking" or "ability grouping"; in its more extreme forms, more often seen overseas, it could be called "Bobbitting." In its less extreme forms it is a classroom management tool, currently coded as "differentiation." Different kids have different capacities for academics, so let those with more capacity move along more quickly and into more complex learning; don't let them get bored. It is understood that given the same time in school, the quicker will get more academics than the slow. Indeed, we give teachers a mandate: "Challenge them all with high expectations that are appropriate to their capacities." And please, heaven help us, have those with less capacity test at least at the "basic" level.

That was then, and understanding society's needs was simpler in the so-called industrial era. This is now, and society's needs are more uncertain, as we are greatly focused on eliminating the "achievement gap" (I call it the "poverty chasm"). Based on the classical subjects, we have Common Core Standards, which have become the official measure of the gap, and schools are mandated to reduce this number, regardless of the unintentional consequences. We make the assumption that capacity for academics is distributed among the population without regard to class, race, or gender, and thus the achievement gap is an artifact of the lower quality of schools in areas of high poverty. There's plenty of evidence that this is true and that the No Child Left Behind law was not, and is not, a fix.

The Harvard Family Research Project states:

> The dominant assumption behind much current educational policy and practice is that school is the only place where and when children learn. This assumption is wrong. Forty years of steadily accumulating research shows that out-of-school, or "complementary learning" opportunities are major predictors of children's development, learning, and educational achievement. The research also indicates that economically and otherwise disadvantaged children are less likely than their more-advantaged peers to have access to these opportunities. This inequity substantially undermines their learning and chances for school success.

There's obviously more to fixing schools than eliminating the achievement gap.

John Falk and Lynn Dierking's "The 95 Percent Solution," published in *American Scientist* Volume 98, Number 6, states that:

> Research by others reinforces that much of what is learned in school actually relates more to learning for school, as opposed to learning for life. One study found that the number or level of mathematics courses taken in school correlated poorly, if at all, with mathematical performance in out-of-school, everyday-life situations. In another study of mathematics learning, even individuals who did not do well or were not formally trained in school mathematics demonstrated the ability to use math successfully in everyday life.

The article, however, makes no mention of an achievement gap for this kind of learning. I was also surprised and amused to find this from an 1860 edition of *Scientific American*:

A child who has been boxed up six hours in school might spend the next four hours in study, but it is impossible to develop the child's intellect in this way. The laws of nature are inexorable. By dint of great and painful labor, the child may succeed in repeating a lot of words, like a parrot, but, with the power of its brain all exhausted, it is out of the question for it to really master and comprehend its lessons. The effect of the system is to enfeeble the intellect even more than the body. We never see a little girl staggering home under a load of books, or knitting her brow over them at eight o'clock in the evening, without wondering that our citizens do not arm themselves at once with carving knives, pokers, clubs, paving stones or any weapons at hand, and chase out the managers of our common schools, as they would wild beasts that were devouring their children.

Are stricter common standards and more hours in school really the only answer, or an answer at all?

"I suppose it is because nearly all children go to school nowadays, and have things arranged for them, that they seem so forlornly unable to produce their own ideas."

—Agatha Christie

"No child on earth was ever meant to be ordinary, and you can see it in them, and they know it, too, but then the times get to them, and they wear out their brains learning what folks expect, and spend their strength trying to rise over those same folks."

—Annie Dillard

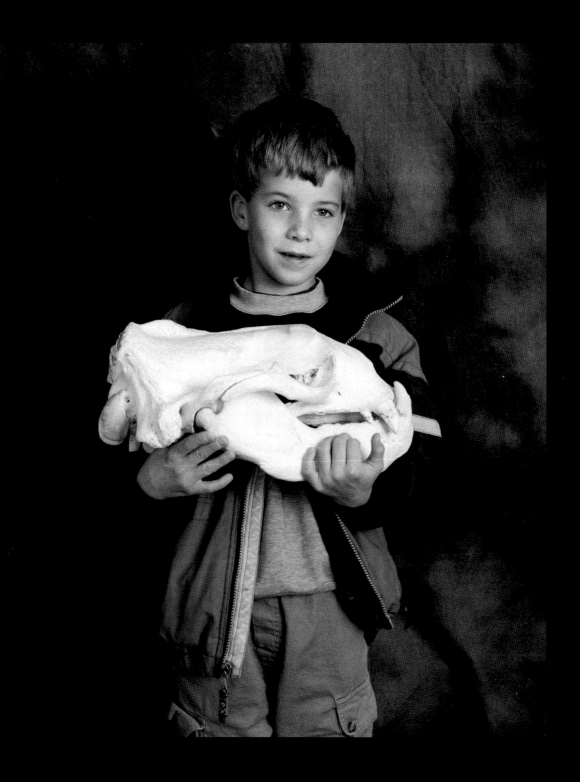

When I get truly interested in a subject I look for the trade journals and ask, What do the practitioners talk about? What are their words, explanations, and ideologies? How do they talk among themselves? My current list of trade journals includes *Educational Leadership*, published by the ASCD (formerly the Association for Supervision and Curriculum Development); *Kappan*, published by Phi Delta Kappa; *American School Board Journal*, published by the National School Boards Association; *Harvard Education Letter*; *Harvard Educational Review*; and *Education Week*. Each, in its own way, offers a peek under the blankets. The March 2011 edition of *Educational Leadership* carries the article "A Diploma Worth Having" by the progressive educator Grant Wiggins. I have selected representative samples that show an intent to get serious about education.

> Students should prepare for adult life by studying subjects that suit their talents, passions, and aspirations as well as needs. They should leave when they are judged to be ready for whatever next challenge they take on— whether it be college, trade school, the military, or playing in a band.

Judged by who and what means? I must ask.

> This plan would enable us to finally deal with the key weakness of high school, summarized in that term virtually all students and adults use to describe it: bor-ing. High school is boring in part because diploma requirements crowd out personalized and engaged learning. It is also boring because our graduation requirements have been produced the way our worst laws are; they are crude compromises, based on inadequate debate. Because of arbitrary policies that define preparation in terms of content instead of useful abilities, schools focus on "coverage," not meaningful learning.

> The Commission on the Reorganization of Secondary Education thought that asking this question was not only sensible but sorely needed—in 1918! Its report "Cardinal Principles of Secondary Education" yielded

a sound set of criteria by which to rationally judge the high school curriculum. The commission underscored that these criteria must flow from the mission of schooling:

> Education in a democracy, both within and without the school, should develop in each individual the knowledge, interests, ideals, habits, and powers whereby he will find his place and use that place to shape both himself and society toward ever nobler ends.

> The Cardinal Principles were a deliberate counterbalance to the policies that had arisen from the work of the Committee of Ten in 1892. That group had famously argued that a college-prep education, including multiple years of Latin and Greek, was appropriate for all students.

Almost sixty years later, in 1949, it took me two years to pass the required Latin requirement; they said it was necessary to improve my vocabulary. I know damn well that talking, listening, reading, and writing are solely responsible for whatever vocabulary I have. Now why, if they were educators, did they lie to me about the value of learning Latin?

> We need to decide to include or exclude, emphasize or deemphasize any subject based on criteria related to school mission—a mission centered on improving the behavior and lives of students. Otherwise, our curricular decisions are arbitrary and school is aimless. Indeed, when we fail to seriously question the inclusion of algebra or the exclusion of ethics from graduation requirements, we can only fall back on custom: "We've always done it this way." But if that were the only real argument, we would still be requiring Greek of all graduates, as the Committee of Ten recommended.

> Our current situation is no better than when the Committee of Ten did its work. Think about it: We are on the verge of requiring every student in

the United States to learn two years of algebra that they will likely never use, but no one is required to learn wellness or parenting.

They will lie to them about the usefulness of algebra just as once they lied to me about Latin. Curses upon educators who lie to their students. As a recent study pointed out, only about 5 percent of the population actually need algebra in their work.

Let us begin a serious national conversation (all of us, not just the policy wonks, selected employers, and college admissions officers) about the questions, What is the point of high school? What do our society and our students need from school, regardless of hidebound tradition or current policy fads?

Frank Sanchez says, "Conversation is a learning style." We need to begin in our kitchens, our churches and our schools, our town halls and our bars, our statehouses, our election campaigns. If we fail to do so, high school will continue to be bor-ing.

"The people you have to lie to, own you. The things
you have to lie about, own you. When your
children see you owned, then they are not your
children anymore, they are the children of what
owns you. If money owns you, they are the children
of money. If your need for pretense and illusion owns
you, they are the children of pretense and illusion.
If your fear of loneliness owns you, they are the
children of loneliness. If your fear of the truth owns
you, they are the children of the fear of truth."

—Michael Ventura

"Life is a wonderful, mysterious adventure,
but the soft nihilism we preach in school
leaves students bored and flaccid."

—Matt McQuines

Jane Roland Martin wrote a wonderful book in 1992 called *The Schoolhome: Rethinking Schools for Changing Families*. She wishes that any child, both at home and school, be wrapped in care, concern, and connections, the "three C's," as she calls them. She argues, from the child's side and in a full, soft, feminine, and progressive moral frame, that this is essential in order for the child to have any chance at achieving a full and effective humanity. She notes that in today's society there are far too many families in which it is unrealistic to expect delivery of the three C's. It is thus doubly important for schools to attend to this gap. Home is the hidden partner in the education of our young, and home is no longer what it once was.

"It is radical conditions which have changed; only an
equally radical change in education suffices."

—John Dewey

Martin suggests that schools must and can adapt; the schoolhouse must become the schoolhome.

"What the best and wisest parent wants for his own child,
that must the community want for all its children."

—John Dewey

"You should do for your children
what their parents fail to do for them."

—Johann Heinrich Pestalozzi

Martin describes some schoolhomes, from Montessori to the Charles River Creative Arts Program to the Atrium School, which are meant to suggest a realm of possibilities. Her hope is that such utopias will naturally replicate themselves. I, too, have seen school utopias; it's good to know that they are indeed possible. It is a great disappointment to me that utopias do not replicate, but instead flower and then wither and die without issue, perhaps of loneliness.

Mike Johnston joined Teach for America, applied for and got the job in Greenville, Mississippi. He was the young, white newbie English teacher in a decaying high school in a decaying neighborhood in a part of the Deep South that has yet to experience any of Martin Luther King Jr.'s dream. He describes this classroom scene in his book *In the Deep Heart's Core*:

> Larry was far more dangerous and enigmatic than Corelle. He had learned to live life physically. I had heard him tell stories about his father's beatings with a mixture of pride and venom. When he was in one of his rages, nothing I could say made any difference to Larry. With a different student I might have put a hand on his shoulder and guided him to his seat, but Larry's rage promised that he would not tolerate my coming anywhere near him.

> The first incident occurred with a scrawny girl who sat in the middle of the room. Shakena was mercilessly ridiculed for being cross-eyed. As a result she had grown up with more than a sizable chip on her shoulder. She had learned that the only way to stop persecution, or to refute it, was to fight. I saw her pick fights with the three largest boys in my room

before she was eventually removed from my class. She would begin with a glare, proceed to a slap or a scratch, and often end in a wild assault of flailing arms, fingernails and feet. Because Larry was always looking for some form of entertainment to make his idle time in my classroom pass more quickly, his attention often lighted on Shakena. In addition to her pugilistic eagerness, Shakena had also developed an ability to zero in on a student's greatest insecurity and bare it for all to see. It was a well-tested method of self-defense. Early in the year she discovered Larry's Achilles' heel: his academic record. Larry had been held back two years in middle school. After spending a year in the alternative school for threatening to kill a teacher, he was promoted to ninth grade without ever passing the eighth.

Young, idealistic Johnston wanted to create a utopia, a schoolhome. What indeed were the possibilities?

Henry Morris describes his vision in his 1924 book *The Village College: Being a Memorandum on the Provision of Educational and Social Facilities for the Countryside, with Special Reference to Cambridgeshire*:

> As the community centre of the neighborhood it would provide for the whole man, and abolish the duality of education and ordinary life. It would not only be the training ground for the art of living, but the place in which life is lived ... The dismal dispute of vocational and non-vocational education would not arise in it. It would be a visible demonstration in stone of the continuity and never ceasingness of education. There would be no "leaving school"! The child would enter at three and leave the college only in extreme old age. It would have the virtue of being local so that it would enhance the quality of actual life as it is lived from day to day ... It would not be divorced from the normal environment of those who would frequent it from day to day, or from that great educational institution, the family ... The Village College could lie athwart the daily lives of the community it serves; and in it the conditions would be

realized under which education would not be an escape from reality, but an enrichment and transformation of it. For education is committed to the view that the ideal order and the actual order can be made one.

Modern U.S. compulsory attendance laws were first enacted in Massachusetts in 1853, and by 1918 all states had compulsory attendance laws. Colorado passed its law in 1889, and it applies to children ages six to seventeen. One reason for these laws was the belief that public school was the best means to improve the literacy rate of the poor and to help assimilate an immigrant population. Another reason was that as children were required to attend school, factory owners found it more difficult to exploit cheap and plentiful child labor, a clear example of the Jeffersonian notion that a universally educated public creates a more healthy and prosperous nation capable of democratic and just self-governance. Later, compulsory schooling was thought to provide the basic skills for employment in the industrial age. Currently the self-governance language has been truncated to "making every child ready for career or college."

There is a certain logical consequence of compulsory schooling, and that is, if governments can and do demand that children go to school, then they can also dictate, by some means or other, what is to go on during those school days. There is dominion over the classroom content, students, and teachers.

"Myths and explanations must be invented to hide domination and present it as something else."

—Paulo Freire

Failure to comply, or truancy, is a misdemeanor in almost every state. The penalties include fines for the first offense, and most states also have the option of sentencing parents for as long as thirty days in jail. Where I live, the Roaring Fork School District policy manual states, "If legal action fails to result in consistent school attendance, a student may, as a last resort, be declared 'habitually truant' and expelled." Paradoxically, the penalty for nonattendance is to be forbidden attendance. Truancy reaches this legal level with four unexcused absences in a month or ten in a year. But wait, state law says every child must be in school, so there is an "Expulsion School" for these truants. It's from 4 to 5 p.m. Monday through Thursday, because who can ask a teacher to work late on Friday afternoon?

Compulsory schooling is the initial act of school bullying; all else follows.

"The purpose of compulsory education is to deprive the common people of their commonsense."

—G. K. Chesterton

"When I am forced by law, my will gives scant assent."

—Terence

"Whatever is exacted by power is ascribed rather to him who commands than to him who executes."

—Valerius Maximus

The dominion of one human over another, or of society over some class or subset, naturally wants to become complete, to allow no leakage—any leakage would be a failure and thus not dominion at all. Thus teachers are the guards of the students, superintendents the guards of the teachers. The public demands the dominion; they are afraid of youth gone wild, or perhaps gone "natural," as Jean-Jacques Rousseau

might call the unschooled. Dominion cannot survive without surveillance, constant surveillance, and all acts of disobedience nipped in the bud.

*"For if we are to dragoon the entire youth popula-
tion into vast prisons in the guise of 'education,' with
teachers and administrators serving as surrogate
wardens and guards, why should we not expect vast
unhappiness, discontent, alienation, and rebellion
on the part of the nation's youth?"*

—Murray Rothbard

*"You cannot have authoritarian tactics to
materialize democratic dreams."*

—Paulo Freire

*"All education is a form of action based on
some kind of social philosophy."*

—Myles Horton

What has it gained us, all these years, that the average test scores of a class, school, or nation are reported as "student achievement"?

Achievement, *n.* 1. Something accomplished, esp. by superior ability, special effort, great courage, etc.; a great or heroic deed.

Or, as Ambrose Bierce defines it: "Achievement, n. The death of endeavor and the birth of disgust."

Leaving aside the sourpuss Bierce, if we had a clear definition of the purposes of school and a way to measure how well students achieved those purposes, it would indeed be great and heroic if students, teachers, and schools measured well.

Test scores a heroic deed? I suggest that we have been spun into desensitivity and a soft acceptance that test scores have some good to them, perhaps even courage, greatness, or heroism. That we don't cry, "Doublespeak!" is strong evidence of the strength and complicity of the giant testing industry, with the whole educational system determined to defend test scores as the only word in describing achievement.

Test scores are indeed an objective, quantitative measure of something about classes, schools, and nations. We all wish that the "something" was understood well enough to determine if they were useful whatsoever in measuring the great and heroic components of purposeful education. But no, what tests measure is simply the student's capacity to circle correct answers. There are many correlations between this capacity and many others that we might associate with true achievement, but no causal relationships. When we use test scores alone to measure student achievement, we have effectively substituted test scores for the whole accountability of public education. We then largely double-speak our way around the intelligent and politically divisive discussion regarding the public purposes of public education.

> Accountable, *adj.* 1. Subject to the obligation to report, explain, or justify; responsible; answerable. To give an account of.

> Account, *n.* 1. An oral or written description of particular events or situations; narrative.

What would an account of a teacher's or student's school year look like? I don't mind if there are some numbers in the narrative, as long as they, too, are accounted for. How much of this accounting have we missed by counting only test scores?

When a parent asks, "What did you do in school today?" and the kid answers, "Nothing," I worry that this is indeed an accurate and complete account all too often.

*"I am entirely certain that twenty years from now
we will look back at education as it is practiced
in most schools today and wonder that we could
have tolerated anything so primitive."*

—JOHN W. GARDNER

*"The way our children learn to see themselves in
schools, first as whole beings and then as dissected
parts ... it has something to do with the windows
we break when we raid their dreams."*

—MARY ELLEN DAKEN

I was in Governor Romer's office to talk about education. It was his last appointment of the day, hence no rush; his mind did not have to be split, planning for the next meeting.

His wife is a teacher and his administration was making education a political platform. He said, "What do you think about raising the floor for education?" I reckoned he was asking, "How do you think it will play with the voters if we frame it as 'raising the floor'?" His assistant brought him a bowl of ice cream with sprinkles; he said it was his afternoon energizer.

I said, "Somehow, when you raise the floor it seems to lower the ceiling." We chatted on about this and that until it was time to leave. Romer's next job was superintendent of Los Angeles Unified School District. I think he would declare that job far more difficult than governor of Colorado.

I think my answer was somehow correct: raising the floor will lower the ceiling; the squeeze is inevitable. The governor and I did not talk about the mechanisms; in other words, just how does raising the floor cause lowering of the ceiling? Well, here's one possible mechanism: raising the floor requires some new demands, public education requires demands be applied equally, and demands require resources that, rather than being added, are diverted from those that allow a higher ceiling. Conjecture: Without additional resources, raising the floor will lower the ceiling.

The "achievement gap" is the focus of the education debate today. "We must reduce the achievement gap"—that's how it's being framed, as an equal rights issue. If raising the floor lowers the ceiling, i.e., reduces that gap, is the converse true, that reducing the gap will raise the floor and lower the ceiling? I think the answer to that one is yes.

Unintended consequences are the norm for complex systems like this thing we call public education.

The federal strategy, as defined in the government's Race to the Top request for proposals, is to raise the floor by turning around or turning out the lowest-ranking

schools, principals, and teachers based upon "student achievement." So it comes down to student achievement, and we move into the arms of the assessment community for this next dance. It won't do anybody any good to have them dance all over our toes, which they are inclined to do.

There *is* such a thing as student achievement, and schools can produce it. We need objective evaluations of the quantity and the quality of the achievement. I argue that objective can, and perhaps must, include qualitative as well as quantitative data. There are many concepts that are complementary to each other, concepts that have a dual. Examples are male/female, being/becoming, hope/fear, etc. I claim that understanding is deeper when descriptions or evaluations include duals. I claim further that *quantitative* has a dual and that it is *qualitative*, and that student achievement will be best understood when both are taken into consideration. I've been poking through some of the journals of the assessment community and haven't caught sight of any duals so far.

We are used to the fact that in a legal trial the jury is presented with much evidence that is not quantitative at all: appearance, body language, intention, remorse. We don't talk about how we might quantify these things; we judge them.

In the United Kingdom, Her Majesty's Inspectorate of Education sends a team into each school for an extended period of observation and delivers its judgments in narrative form to the school and to the rest of the world.

"If we try to keep our children within safe boundaries,
we prevent them from undertaking any
great experiment with Truth."

—Parker Palmer

"The schools are a public institution oriented to equality in a society dominated by private institutions oriented to the market."

—Daniel K. Cohen and Barbara Neufeld

Schools almost always declare that they offer, and often demand, "rigorous academics," and parents almost always say, "Good. That's just what I want for my child." Let's just take apart the words: "Rigorous" owns the synonyms "stern," "austere," "hard," "inflexible," "stiff," and "unyielding." "Academic, 1. Of or pertaining to an institution of higher learning," but also, "4. Learned or scholarly but lacking in worldliness, common sense, or practicality." You can put the words together as you see fit; for me it's "stiff impracticalities."

Standards have become the measure of rigorous academics. The 2002 No Child Left Behind federal legislation required all states to adopt standards and to create tests to determine if the standards are met by their schools. The states did this, and even became competitive in the degree of rigor, which they sometimes call stiffness, as in "stiff standards." The race becomes a silliness of "Mine's stiffer'n yours."

In early 2009 the U.S. Department of Education encouraged a voluntary forty-eight-state consortium of the National Governors Association and the Council of Chief State School Officers to draft Common Core State Standards in mathematics and English language arts. Incredibly, they did this in about twelve months, and equally incredibly, it is likely that almost all states will adopt these standards. We will essentially have a set of national educational standards, just like almost all the rest of the developed countries.

As an example, here is the kind of eighth-grade math mastery deemed essential: "Understand that the patterns of association can also be seen as bivariate categorical data by displaying frequencies and relative frequencies in a two-way table." I asked our town mayor, who is also an architect, if he found this essential; he said he didn't understand a word that I said. Here's an eighth-grade language arts standard: "Write arguments in which they: Introduce a claim about a topic or issue, distinguish it from alternate or opposing claims, and organize the reasons and evidence logically to support the claim. Support the claim with logical reasoning and detailed and relevant evidence from credible sources to demonstrate a comprehensive understanding of the topic." I applied my red scoring pencil to a sample of *New York Times* columnists' work. You might want to try that exercise too.

"What does education do? It makes a straight-cut
ditch out of a free, meandering brook."

—HENRY DAVID THOREAU

"When one considers in its length and breadth
the importance of a nation's young, the broken
lives, the defeated hopes, the national failures,
which result from the frivolous inertia with
which education is treated, it is difficult to
restrain within oneself a savage rage."

—ALFRED NORTH WHITEHEAD

Higher education, or post-secondary education, is an interesting cultural and economic institution. The standard assumption is that one's education is complete with a degree from a college or university, incomplete without this degree. The historic economic data show that completion has hugely increased lifetime earnings, and thus the time spent in college was well-spent in terms of financial return for money and time invested. At least as far as the money spent for higher education, the employer, over time, pays the student back for it, and thus effectively pays for the college experience. As far as the time spent for higher education is concerned, we have little data on what the return is. The time spent is sanctioned, anyway, in the United Nations International Covenant on Economic, Social and Cultural Rights of 1966, Article 13: "Higher education shall be made equally accessible to all, on the basis of capacity, by every appropriate means, and in particular by the progressive introduction of free education."

In the forty-five years since, the costs of higher education have increased faster than the Consumer Price Index; so much for free. There are now multiple financial institutions that finance the nonwealthy student's higher education; "School now, pay later." It's like a mortgage on a house, except there's no house as an asset to collateralize the loan; there's just the *assumption* that the employer will pay a premium such that the loan is paid off.

Assumptions are a scary kind of collateral. "It's a sure thing. You can't go wrong buying a tulip, a house, a college degree." We just found out that when real estate values stagnate or decrease there is a mortgage crisis that shakes our whole financial system. We humans have an interesting history with market bubbles: trade at prices that are at considerable variance with intrinsic values. Because it is often difficult to determine intrinsic values in real-life markets, bubbles are often identified only in retrospect, when a sudden drop in prices appears, when the bubble bursts.

> *"Faith may be defined briefly as an illogical belief in the occurrence of the improbable."*
>
> —H. L. Mencken

There are market values and there are intrinsic values. Today the price of a gallon of gasoline is 5 percent above (or below) where it was a month ago, yet a gallon will take me precisely the same distance. Its intrinsic value is unchanged; it gets me where I want to go. Can we lay out the intrinsic value of a college degree? How is it the wherewithal to get us where we want to go?

"Some people get an education without going to
college; the rest get it after they get out."

—Mark Twain

"Every man should have a college education to show
him how little the thing is really worth."

—Elbert Hubbard

I've gotten into the annoying habit of asking friends and acquaintances, "When was the last time that you actually used algebra because it was important to your life?" The answer is pretty universally "tenth grade," or whenever they completed their last algebra course in high school. I take it that algebra is not a life skill, and if it is a job skill for some very few professions, then it can be learned as part of that professional training.

The 2003 National Assessment of Adult Literacy was administered by the U.S. Department of Education to more than 19,000 adults (ages sixteen and older) living in households or prisons. It examined prose literacy, document literacy, and quantitative literacy. Quantitative literacy is described as "the knowledge and skills needed to identify and perform computations using numbers that are embedded in printed materials." Literacy was measured "directly by tasks representing a range of literacy activities that adults are likely to face in their daily lives."

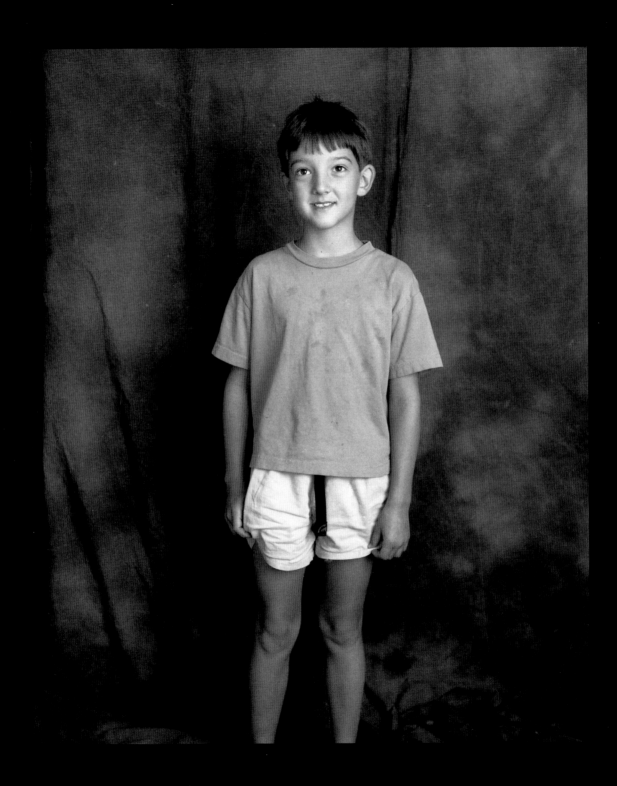

Here are basic quantitative literacy exercises from the assessment, shown in ascending level of difficulty:

- Calculate the cost of a sandwich and a salad using prices from a menu.
- Locate two numbers in a bar graph and calculate the difference between them.
- Calculate the weekly salary for a job based on hourly wages listed in a job advertisement.
- Perform a two-step calculation to find the cost of three baseball tickets using an order form that gives the price of one ticket and the postage and handling charge.

Some samples of intermediate quantitative literacy, also shown according to difficulty:

- Determine what time a person can take a prescription medication based on information on the prescription drug label that relates timing of medication to eating.
- Calculate the total cost of ordering office supplies using a page from an office supply catalog and an order form.
- Determine whether a car has enough gasoline to get to the next gas station based on a graphic of the car's fuel gauge, a sign stating the miles to the next gas station, and information given about the car's fuel use.
- Calculate the cost of raising a child for a year in a family with a specified income based on a newspaper article that provides the percentage of a typical family's budget that goes toward raising children.

And here are sample proficient quantitative literacy questions from the assessment:

- Calculate the yearly cost of a specified amount of life insurance using a table that gives cost per month for each $1,000 of coverage.
- Determine the number of units of flooring required to cover the floor in a room when the area of the room is not evenly divisible by the unit in which the flooring is sold.
- Calculate an employee's share of health insurance costs for a year using a table that shows how the employee's monthly cost varies with income and family size.

Whoa, don't crowd me now, I'm about to give you the results for the American public school system, which is now trying to add a second year of algebra to its graduation requirements.[3]

Race/ethnicity	Percent proficient	Percent below basic
White	17%	13%
Black	2%	47%
Hispanic	4%	50%
Asian	12%	19%
Native American	10%	32%

Your Honor, we rest our case. Eighty-seven percent of these adults have graduated from high school; 39 percent have a college degree. Tell me what this means about how well we retain and use all that math so earnestly and intently shoved down our throats?

3. For a full report, see: nces.ed.gov/pubs2007/2007480.pdf.

*"Teaching school is but another word for sure
and not very slow destruction."*

—Thomas Carlyle

I assume that the television industry has a very good understanding of what its audience likes to watch. My informal survey of what characters, settings, and formats are often presented: cops and robbers, hospital emergency rooms, reality shows, lawyers and courts, high school social dramas, and canned laughter sitcoms. Few of us have been cops or robbers, ER doctors, stranded on an island with mean people, or lawyers, defendants, or plaintiffs in court; our lives are a sitcom without canned laughter, and the majority of us have gone to high school. I take it that the painful dramas of high school social life strike some kind of resonance among viewers, more so than, say, their classroom learning experiences.

I have become interested in the public misunderstanding of public education as possibly the root cause of the failure of school reform. If the public truly understood it, they simply wouldn't stand for the sad shape of such a critical institution. A Phi Delta Kappa/Gallup poll that grades American schools is presented in the September 2010 issue of the *Kappan* magazine. The 2010 survey findings are based on 1,008 interviews with a national sample of adults eighteen and older drawn from the Gallup Panel. Following are some selections:

> Using the A, B, C, D, and FAIL scale, what grade would you give the
> school your oldest child attends?
>
> | | |
> |---|---|
> | A | 36% |
> | B | 41% |
> | A & B | 77% |

What grade would you give the public schools in the nation as a whole?

A	1%
B	17%
A & B	18%

Ah, I get it! In a nation of local control by local school boards, the only schools that I *could* influence don't need my help. Good, I can get back to my TV show. Though not part of this poll, most adults rate the schools that *they* attended as of high quality, and they regard themselves as well-educated.

The following questions were also asked in the Phi Delta Kappa/Gallup poll:

How would you rate the overall impact of No Child Left Behind on public schools in your community?

Helping	22%
Making no difference	45%
Hurting	28%

How do you suppose teachers would answer the questions below, as opposed to the parents who did?

Which is a more important factor in determining whether students learn in school?

The school	22%
The parents	76%

Do you have trust and confidence in the men and women who are teaching children in the public schools?

Yes	71%
No	27%

Teachers are handed down standards, curricula, and tests. They are trusted only insofar as their students' test scores prove that they have done what they have been told to do. Apparently some 71 percent of parents believe teachers are living up to this standard.

Do we agree that the public understanding of public education is as low as the public understanding of national and international finance? Is it a higher priority issue, worth a real effort, even though it will be hard? What would that effort look like? How do we involve the public education system, the government, the media? How is that effort powered?

> *"The schools will surely be failures if students*
> *graduate knowing how to choose the right option*
> *from four bubbles on a multiple-choice test,*
> *but unprepared to lead fulfilling lives, to be*
> *responsible citizens, and to make good choices*
> *for themselves, their families, and our society."*
>
> —Diane Ravitch

Evolution is often summarily described as "survival of the fittest," quick and dirty, and certainly more positive than the equivalent, "extinction for the unfit." Wars, pestilence, and famine are all too frequent spikes in a steady state of grind-'em-down-in-poverty form of extinction.

> *"The greatest of our evils and the*
> *worst of crimes is poverty."*
>
> —George Bernard Shaw

Historically we do not usually set out to directly impoverish folks; we shrug and accept that the less fit will naturally have to do with less, and the best we could or should do about it is offer them "alms for the poor" and get on about our business.

My mother used to say, "Them that has, gets, them that hasn't, doesn't." She was no Bible reader, but …

"For unto every one that hath shall be given, and he shall have abundance; but from him that hath not shall be taken away even that which he hath."

—Matthew 25:29

J. J. Rousseau analyzed the situation this way:

> The first man who had fenced in a piece of land, said, "This is mine," and found people naïve enough to believe him, that man was the true founder of civil society. From how many crimes, wars, and murders, from how many horrors and misfortunes might not anyone have saved mankind, by pulling up the stakes, or filling up the ditch, and crying to his fellows: Beware of listening to this imposter; you are undone if you once forget that the fruits of the earth belong to us all, and the earth itself to nobody.

Indeed, "this is mine" means that it is not yours; and we, too often, will defend that forever, for me and mine against you and yours. Those who are late to the "this is mine" table get the scraps or alms. Poverty seems to just come along with the human condition, from each of us living our self-interests.

There are those who declare this acceptance to be cruel, merciless, unjust, even inhumane. Lyndon B. Johnson, shortly after passing the Elementary and Secondary

Education Act (ESEA) in 1965, spoke to a high school class: "Neither you nor I are willing to accept the tyranny of poverty, not the dictatorship of ignorance, nor the despotism of ill health, nor the oppression of bias and prejudice and bigotry." The ESEA was Johnson's mobilization of federal power in his war on poverty. Its major thrust was its Title I financial assistance to local schools for the education of low-income children. The ESEA has been continuously reauthorized ever since, and always with care to avoid anything that might be interpreted as national standards or curriculum. The feds entered the education system in the name of civil rights, not with what or how children are to be taught, which traditionally, and probably constitutionally, belongs to the states. The latest edition of the ESEA was passed in 2002 under the name No Child Left Behind, and it is due to be reauthorized by the current Congress.

During most of the twentieth century, public education assessed itself by the quality of its inputs: facilities, teacher credentials, seat time, and curriculum as determined by states and local school districts. By these measures, it was clear that the War on Poverty had been lost in public schooling: inputs were, and still are, dreadfully unequal between haves and have-nots. Sometime around the late eighties the educational leadership shifted: "Why do we worry about inputs? It's objective outputs that count; only outputs can gauge progress on educating all of our children equally and well." Given that the nation does not trust a teacher's opinion, the only objective evidence, and cheap enough too, are standardized tests. Numbers, God bless 'em, not mumbles from the mouths of teachers.

The NCLB Act, carefully avoiding any hint of national standards or curriculum, demanded that every state adopt its own standards, devise tests to those standards, and report the data disaggregated by race, class, ethnicity, etc. The difference in scores between rich and poor is now called the "achievement gap," and there are punishments assigned to schools that don't improve overall and at the same time reduce the achievement gap. The presumption is that faced with the punishment, schools would learn to adjust their inputs. We should not be surprised that the achievement gap remains, and exactly reflects the continued discrepancy of inputs.

This Congress is due to reauthorize the ESEA that technically expired in 2007. We hear early talk of a return to making sure that the inputs, defined now simply as the teachers, are good and equitably provided. How will we know if a teacher is a good input? Exactly by the output as measured by test scores. It's well-known that teaching in have-not schools is very hard work, and now you can be fired for trying.

"Healthy nations have healthy schools, it's not the other way around." John Goodlad got this right, and it will do no good shaking our fingers at teachers and schools for not making it right.

Has our education system in any way prepared our youth for the new normal, the complex, hot, crowded, and flat world of this century? In examining the Common Core Standards, what it supposedly takes to be career and college ready in the twenty-first century, I notice that one requirement includes reading and understanding *The Great Gatsby*, when what we really need is to hear and understand our neighbors' stories. Another requirement demands that students "Represent addition, subtraction, multiplication and conjugation of complex numbers geometrically on the complex plane; use properties of this representation for computation. *For example*, $(-1 + \sqrt{3}\,i)^3$ = 8 *because* $(-1 + \sqrt{3}\,i)$ *has modulus 2 and argument 120°*," when what we really need is to calculate how we can provide more energy to the world's poorest without tipping the climate. It's not, and it never was, about complex numbers; it's about a complex society slipping away from our grip.

Zoe Weil claims that a humane education offers accurate information about the challenges of our times so students have the knowledge on which to base solutions. What, when, and how will we tell our children about this?

Nature or nurture used to be a way of finding simple answers as to why we are the way we are.

You might say, "Oh, she's got a temper just like her father. She got it from him; it's in her genes." Or, alternatively, "She observed and absorbed how well her father's temper allowed him to get his way, and so she figured, 'I can do that too, just like Dad.'" In the second case, we would say it was in her memes.

Richard Dawkins invented the word "meme" in his 1976 book, *The Selfish Gene*, to explain the propagation and staying power of ideas, values, patterns of behavior, and cultural phenomena that are spread by nongenetic means. Dawkins used examples such as melodies, catchphrases, beliefs, clothing/fashion, and the technology of building arches.

Memes reside in our social structures, particularly those structures that are enduring and/or traditional. A social structure that endures has developed internal patterns of behavior, or memes, designed for survival. Since social structures do adapt to a changing world, Dawkins believed that memes, like genes, also mutate. Indeed, we still use the metaphor "social structure as life" when we talk about birth, growth, power, age, and death of a social structure.

One meme is the social construct of childhood, the idea that there is a period of time between infancy and adulthood that is somehow different. It takes a pretty well-developed idea of what childhood is to think through how society deals with this state. The histories of these ideas and of schools are quite parallel. In our Western tradition, the idea of schools traces to ancient Greece, when Plato popularized the concept of compulsory education at the same time as proposing that children be straightened out by "threats and blows, like a piece of warped wood." This brutish idea of childhood, along with any ideas at all of schools, disappeared with the fall of the Roman Empire, the Dark Ages, and then the Middle Ages.

The social structures significantly associated with teaching and learning include families, clans or tribes, churches, schools, and formal and informal voluntary associations. The list is ordered approximately according to their significance as the child develops into adulthood. I am interested here in the structures called schools. In particular I'm interested in public schools, where "public" means "subject to the public will because of funding by broad-based taxation." It's fair to call public schools an institution. In fact, the dictionary definition of "school" is "*n.* an institution where instruction is given."

Schools existed long before there were public schools. Interestingly, the word "school" derives from the Greek for "leisure" and "that in which leisure is employed." Of course! For most of the world and for most of history, children were part of the labor force. It took the development of economies that did not require child labor for schools to be available to any child; before, the privileged were the only ones who could command such a thing as leisure.

"To school" is also a verb meaning "to instruct, stabilize, or inure by practice, long or repeated experience, or subjection to systemic discipline." I ask people for their story about what "school" means to them. My own story begins with Mrs. Lewis in kindergarten, or what I refer to as my unschooled mind's first meeting with the institution. Mrs. Lewis was formidable, large and commanding, and subjected us to systemic discipline. "You may not start a new play-project unless and until you have put away properly your old project." I was building a fantasy cabin out of Lincoln Logs and left my unfinished project to get some more of the flat green strips I needed from the Lincoln Logs box. Mrs. Lewis descended on me—"You may not start a new project until you have put away your old project"—and I returned my incomplete cabin to the shelf. I knew then that school was not a place that cared for me, that was concerned and connected to me. My unschooled mind does not forget this incident. I had already experienced discipline within my family; now I understood it within a school: you are not free to build the cabin of your dreams.

Neil Postman writes,

> The institution we call "school" is what it is because we made it that way. If it is irrelevant, as Marshall McLuhan says; if it shields children from reality, as Norbert Wiener says; if it educates for obsolescence, as John Gardner says; if it does not develop intelligence, as Jerome Bruner says; if it is based on fear, as John Holt says; if it avoids the promotion of significant learnings, as Carl Rogers says; if it induces alienation, as Paul Goodman says; if it punishes creativity and independence, as Edgar Friedenberg says; if, in short, it is not doing what needs to be done, it can be changed; it *must* be changed.

"The philosophy of the school room in one generation will be the philosophy of the government in the next."

—Abraham Lincoln

"Dare the schools create a new social order?"

—Joe Nathan

Schools are institutions and part of a school *system* that responds to many social needs and forces beyond education. The governance of the system has evolved in response to these many needs and forces, and consequently often makes decisions where education is not the highest priority. For high school there is the need to prepare students for college and a career, for middle school the need to prepare students for high school, and so on down the grades. This leads to schooling driven by the goal of meeting the entrance requirements of college. There is the need to have standardized test results come out as high as possible and with no gap between scores of different races or classes. There is sometimes a need to have winning athletic teams. In suburban schools there is a need that they be "nice"; besides bright and well-decorated classrooms and a groovy no-drunks senior prom, "nice" can mean textbooks and curricula that do not offend any significant portion of the community. Particularly in urban schools there is the need to eliminate guns, to reduce teenage pregnancies and drug use, and the need to keep kids in schools rather than on the streets in gangs.

There is a more complex national need that is imposed on public education. Public schools are regulated to conform to the current paradigm of American democracy, somehow blanketing the spectrum of conservative to progressive. There is federal funding for free or reduced-cost meals for the poor, laws that require equal educational opportunity for the disabled and for those with limited proficiency in English, and on and on. We make our commitment to universal education at a time when the diversity of students entering the public schools has never been greater, and when the other institutions that in the past shared responsibility for educating and socializing the next generation—families, churches, and communities—are struggling. As these traditional institutions have faltered, schools have been called upon to cope with the most difficult problems of the larger society and to pay more and more attention to students' nonacademic needs.

A typical teacher's manual may weigh five pounds, and it's not about what to teach or how to teach; it's about complying with regulations and meeting the needs described above. A typical superintendent is expected to know as much as a decent lawyer about a school's exposure to lawsuits, from an infringement of a student's or teacher's right to equal treatment under current law.

The major textbook publishers sell their series to schools not based on educative value, but based on the textbook's ability to meets all the state and federal guidelines and requirements, as well as the district curriculum, and there should be nothing offensive to any extremist group in it whatsoever. Does this explain a neglect of any serious critical analysis of astrology?

Make no mistake, in no way am I saying that equal rights and equal opportunity are not good for schools. Schools need to model democracy and compassion. I am saying that restrictions and regulations can be bad for education.

A third-grade teacher in Michigan told me, "I spend 80 percent of my time teaching the kids where to put their galoshes and not to hold hands or sing in the halls."

A superintendent told me, "If I didn't have SATs in my life, I would run an entirely different school."

A middle-school principal said, "I go to ten to fifteen meetings a week, and never do we talk about the needs of children."

> *"Instead of evaluating schools in terms of long-term effects on their alumni, which appear to be relatively uniform, we think it wiser to evaluate schools in terms of their immediate effects on teachers and students, which appear much more variable. Some schools are dull, depressing, even terrifying places, while others are lively, comfortable, and reassuring. If we think of school life as an end in itself rather than a means in some other end, such differences are enormously important. Eliminating these differences would not do much to make adults more equal, but it would do a great deal to make the quality of children's (and teachers') lives more equal. Since children are in school for a fifth of their lives, this would be a significant accomplishment."*
>
> —Seymour Sarason

There is what we describe as the "core" conceptualization of the classroom: teachers teach from the front of the room, deciding what is to be learned, in what manner, and under what conditions. The primary means of grouping for instruction is the entire class. The major daily classroom activities are the teacher telling, explaining, and questioning students while the students listen, answer, read, and write. Seatwork or supervised study is an extension of these activities.

There is a "core" belief about the nature of teaching and learning, that knowledge is discrete bits of information about particular subjects and that student learning is the acquisition of this information through processes of repetition, memorization, and regular testing of recall. The teacher is the center of the classroom, initiates most of the talk, and orchestrates most of the interaction in the classroom.

The "core" also includes structural arrangements of schools, such as the physical layout of classrooms, student grouping practices, teachers' responsibilities for groups of students, and relationships among teachers in their work with students, as well as processes for assessing student learning and communicating it to students, teachers, parents, administrators, and other interested parties.

Tinkering with the core is as old as schools themselves, and the record is roughly this: any commonsense, humane variation from the core results in improved learning as measured by any commonsense, humane method of measurement. We have also learned that variations do not last long and do not go to scale. Teachers who tinker gather together in ways that cut them off from contact and connection with those who find ambitious teaching intimidating and unfeasible. We know that powerful ideas can change practices in a small fraction of settings but continue to fail in moving those practices beyond the group of teachers who are intrinsically motivated and competent to engage in them. The innovators, left alone as they are, soon either leave or return to the core.

The core of schooling remains relatively stable in the face of significant and ongoing changes in the structures that surround it. Schools legitimize themselves with their various conflicting populations by constantly changing external structures and processes while shielding their workers from any fundamental impact resulting from these changes by leaving the core intact. This accounts for the resilience of practice within the context of constant institutional change.

The expectation that teachers will maintain order is one of the few expectations for which staff associate and anticipate professional consequences. Unsuccessful teachers are asked to leave when their classrooms appear "crazy" or when administrators have to intervene frequently. Teachers know they are doing a good job when their classrooms and the halls are quiet and when administrators do not have to intervene. Such order teaches children how to behave in society, which is necessary for them to be successful.

Schools develop their own internal normative structures that are relatively immune to external influences, and teaching is an essentially isolated occupation in which teachers are left largely to their own devices.

I often hear public apathy about education expressed like this: "This is the way it was for me, I'm educated, this is the way it's supposed to be, and I have a lot of other stuff to worry about." The classroom exists as an isolated core in a system designed to not just accept that state but to protect it, in a society that is not willing to undertake the considerable effort to change things. The core is known, trusted, and totally under control—we know what's happening to our kids, and hey, c'mon, it's not that bad …

"School learning is just learning school."

—Etienne Wenger

George Lakoff in the *Political Mind*[4] describes conservative and liberal beliefs in terms of two different moral structures.

Conservative thought begins with the notion that morality is obedience to an authority, assumed to be a legitimate authority that is inherently good, knows right from wrong, functions to protect us from evil in the world, and has both the right and duty to use force to command obedience and fight evil. Obedience to legitimate authority requires both personal responsibility and discipline, which are prime conservative virtues. Obedience is enforced through punishment.

For the authority to know right from wrong, there must be an absolute right and wrong, and that means that categories must be absolute. Relativism and gray areas are unwelcomed by conservatives.

Competition is crucial. It builds discipline. Without competition, without the desire to win, no one would have the incentive to be disciplined, and morality would suffer. Not everyone can win in a competition, only the most disciplined people, who are also the most morally worthy. Winning is thus a sign of being deserving, of being a good person. Conservative families often promote competitive sports and take them very seriously.

Our framework of a "classroom core" is a near perfect expression of conservative morals. The teacher is a legitimate authority who is to be obeyed, or else. Essentially everything learned, knowledge or skills, is either absolutely right or wrong. Papers are returned with either Cs or Xs; grades are numbers without error bars. Competition is everywhere—for grades, for teacher favor, rising to the fury of high school competitive sports, of which wrestling, where to compete is to inflict pain, is my least favorite.

In first grade, Mrs. Smith announced, "Let's have a spelling contest. Who can spell skwurel?" Barbara Johnston, the math teacher's daughter, without raising her hand to be called on, as I had, spelled out s-q-u-i-r-r-e-l. "Oh, that is so good! Now let's get out our spelling books." I kept my hand up for a few moments longer before opening the spelling book in defeat. Kids are wounded in school in many subtle ways.

4. See also Lakoff's *Moral Politics.*

Why do conservatives want schools to teach to the test and make judgments on the basis of test scores? To determine merit, who deserves to move up into the stratosphere of merit versus who gets to serve people of merit. That should be determined by discipline, punishment, and obedience, learning answers by rote, with punishment for failing to do so as an incentive to be more disciplined next time. We learn what we do, and students that "do" school, engaging with it as it is, learn to be conservative.

"Thou shalt not covet, but tradition
Approves all forms of competition."

—A. H. Clough

"When a nation's young men are conservative,
its funeral bell is already rung."

—Henry Ward Beecher

Lakoff uses two profoundly different sociologies of families to illustrate the divergent moral worldviews of conservatives and liberals: a strict father family for conservatives and a nurturing parent family for liberals. In the ideal strict-father family, the world is seen as a dangerous place and the father functions as protector from "others"; he is the parent who teaches children absolute right from wrong, true from false, by punishing them when they do wrong. The father is the ultimate authority; children are to work hard and do as they are told. Not to do so is immoral and will not, and should not, come to anything but a bad ending. Competition is viewed as the primary route to success. Conservatives place the highest value on protecting and extending the conservative moral system itself.

Ideal liberal families are based on nurturance, which breaks down into empathy, responsibility—for both oneself and others—and excellence: doing as well as one can

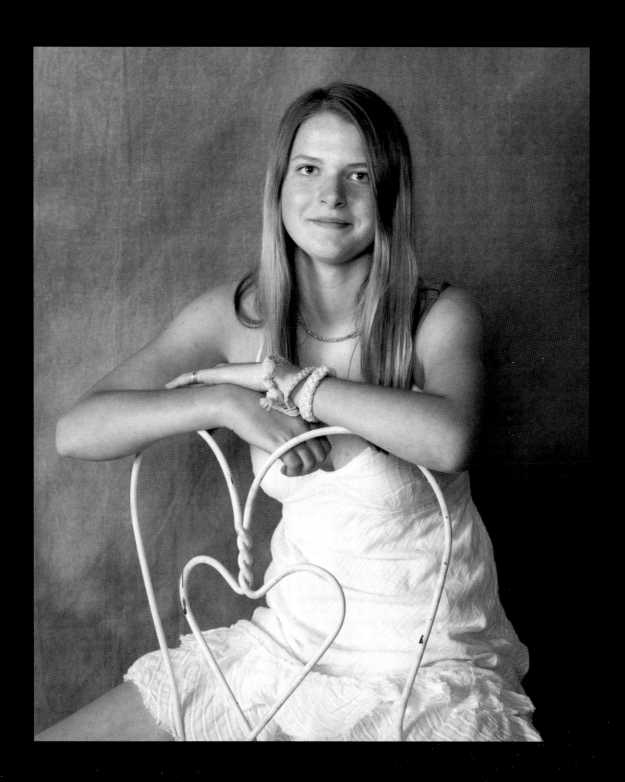

to make oneself better and one's family and community better. Parents are to practice these things, and children are to learn them by example. Collaboration is viewed as the primary route to success. The ideal liberal family also perceives the world as dangerous, but faces this danger with the attitude, "We've got to work together and take care of each other."

Because our first experience with governance begins in our families, we all learn a basic metaphor: "A governing institution is a family." Later, the governing institution may actually be a church, a school, a team, or a nation, yet we understand each as a generalization of family.

A school is a governing institution, and public schools, by virtue of public funding, are political governing institutions based on morality. Political leaders all make proposals they deem right. No one proposes a policy they deem wrong. But there are two opposing moral systems at work in America. Which moral system you are using governs how you will see the world and the "right" role for schools within it.

History has generated a largely conservative moral system for schools and their governance. The strict schoolmarm replaces the strict father, otherwise the values are the same: work hard and do as you are told; anything else is wrong, immoral, and bound to end up badly. Competition is ubiquitous within and between schools. The teacher punishes those who are wrong, the school punishes the teachers who are wrong, and the district punishes the schools that are wrong. Public education is deeply rooted in conservative moral politics.

Within this moral worldview we frame a "good" class: the students are at their desks, on task as directed by the teacher, who has selected the task because if they work hard and do as they are told it will be "good" for them. The students understand and agree to that premise. They compete for an intangible called "grades." As long as this remains the framework of the good classroom, we have accepted the conservative moral politics of public education.

Note that the popular media universally presents this framework for the good classroom, and presents standardized test scores as "student achievement." It is not uncommon to find folks who are liberal on most other issues to be conservative on education, especially as almost all of us attended a strict-father school. It's commonplace that most Americans declare that public education is a mess and needs fixing while their and their children's education is just fine. When asked why their local school is exceptional, they give a knowing grin and say, "Of course, we are an exceptional community."

Teachers don't become teachers because they want to change schools. They liked school, they liked their classes and their teachers, and that's why they became teachers.

American history is founded upon a concept of freedom that has high moral value to both conservatives and liberals. However, the concept is understood differently by the two: the conservative frames freedom as "leave me alone," the liberal as "liberty with justice for all" or "do no harm." When it comes to their children, both conservatives and liberals demand the absolute right to bring up their children within their conservative or liberal moral values without challenge. As such, America has handed most control over education to the local school districts as opposed to the state or federal governments.

Richard F. Elmore, professor of educational leadership at the Harvard Graduate School of Education, describes it this way:

> There is no political discipline among elected officials and their advisors. To policymakers, every idea about what schools should be doing is as credible as every other idea, and any new idea that can command a political constituency can be used as an excuse for telling schools to do something. Elected officials—legislators, governors, mayors, school board members—generate electoral credit by initiating new ideas, not by making the kind of steady investments in people that are required to make the education sector more effective. The result is an education sector that is overwhelmed by policy, conditioned to respond to the immediate

demands of whoever controls the political agenda, and not invested in the long-term health of the sector and the people who work in it.

This condition seems to be a result of our particularly American form of political pluralism. It is not—I repeat *not*—the case in the other industrialized democracies in which I work, Canada and Australia. My own diagnosis is that this condition is a consequence of an extremely weak professional culture in American schools. Policymakers do not have to respect the expertise of educators, because there are no political consequences attached to that lack of respect.

*"Rewards and punishments are
the lowest form of education."*

—Chuang-Tzu

"You're either with us or against us." On, Off. Black, White. True, False. "Just Say No." No, there are no easy answers, no simple solutions, and there are always all the shades of gray between the extremes. Like everything, competition comes in degrees, a continuum, from hard to soft, from conservative to liberal. Hard competition is like boxing or wrestling: there is victory and defeat, dominator and dominated, and the loser may experience pain and/or humiliation. In hard competition there can be no winner without a loser. Soft competition occurs when we compare our strengths in order to position ourselves in the most optimal fashion within our community, continually striving toward a higher purpose. You throw the football the best, so you play quarterback; the good news is that I'm better at blocking anyway.

School is a lot about competition, and primarily of the harder nature. It's not just the wrestling team, it's the valedictorian, the prom queen, the spelling bee champion, and on and on. In fact, student academic achievement, however measured, is historically a matter of competition: students compete for grades and college entrance. Competition that has winners and losers is inherently violent. Not always blood and guts violence, but of the nature described by Kirsten Olson in *Wounded by School: Recapturing the Joy in Learning and Standing Up to Old School Culture.*

I propose that healthy classrooms and healthy schools choose nonviolence as the foundation of health and look to eliminate violence even if it means reexamining the role of competition. What might society look like if our children spent their school time learning through cooperation? I know that the human species' evolutionary success is a product of our great and oftentimes hard competitive capacity, but is there any reason to carry that into childhood and schools?

Martin Luther King Jr.'s 1963 March on Washington required marchers to sign a pledge of nonviolence. Stripped of the religious proscriptions, they included:

2. Remember the nonviolent movement seeks justice and reconciliation—not victory.

5. Sacrifice personal wishes that all might be free.

6. Observe with friend and foes the ordinary rules of courtesy.

7. Perform regular service for others and the world.

8. Refrain from violence of fist, tongue, and heart.

You know, I've never seen this kind of stuff in the mission statements of schools or school districts, homeowners associations … or anywhere else …

"In violence we forget who we are."

—Mary McCarthy

"Violence can only be concealed by a lie, and the lie can only be maintained by violence. Any man who has once proclaimed violence as his method is inevitably forced to take the lie as his principle."

—Alexander Solzhenitsyn

We humans are usually pleased to enumerate and compartmentalize things: the Ten Commandments, the Eightfold Way, the Three Rs, the Seven Intelligences, and so on. I challenged Howard Gardner once on his propensity to compartmentalize intelligence into seven forms. He answered that "it's best to carve the bird at its proper joints." He agreed that his way wasn't the only way, just the proper way, simple and good enough to be useful as a practical matter. I fell into this practice once while indoctrinating some new teachers into life at the Aspen Community School. I declared that there were four principal purposes and named them: lifelong learning, responsibility, community, and social justice.

We discussed lifelong learning as "I don't really care if you read by third grade; I care that you read for the rest of your life." Responsibility as "If we tell you what and how to do it, we have stolen from you your responsibility to figure that out for yourselves." Community as "We know each other and we care for each other, we have common higher purpose, we share it among ourselves, and we care for our wounded." Lunch hour came before we got much further than "Injustices are harmful, and we are committed to doing no harm."

I was explaining these four "directions" to Cliff, a fine middle-school principal, who immediately jumped on it. "Describe this thing you call social justice," he said. I answered that we each have our individual sets of what we call injustices, and social justice is the set that includes none of these. I cannot defend this definition as being good enough to be useful as a practical matter. Upon some reflection I think a better answer might have been that social justice is simply what's intuitively fair. Out in the big adult world, justice is codified within written laws and prescribed punishments, and at least half of the people I know who have gotten entangled in it have said, "It's not fair."

I listened to Vivian Gussin Paley talk about her book *You Can't Say You Can't Play*. A gentleman asked at the end, "Everybody knows the world is not fair and so why pretend?" Paley pulled herself up an extra inch and said, "But aren't schools one place where we *try* to be fair?"

School is about learning, and learning is about doing; we learn what we do. If justice is what is to be learned, then justice must be what the school *does*. Just as school *produces* lifelong learning, takes responsibility, and *builds* community, it *does* justice. "Do justice, love mercy," Micah 6:8. Claus Offe and Ulrich Preuss in "Democratic Institutions and Moral Response," a chapter in David Held's *Political Theory Today*, suggest that this requires "an open-ended and continuous learning process in which the roles of 'teacher' and 'curriculum' are missing. In other words, what is to be learned is a matter we must settle in the process of learning itself."

In a democratic school, everyone affected by a decision has the opportunity to participate in that decision. Such schools usually have a justice system that involves the whole school meeting together. Those who claim an injustice present their case at the meeting, and the group decides, by vote if necessary, how to redress the injustice and erase the harm, hopefully forever. Justice is learned, not just received. *Democratic Schools: Lessons in Powerful Education*, edited by Michael Apple and James Beane, is an excellent resource for this model, and the thirty schools in the Sudbury Valley School franchise are living examples.

The Alpine Valley School is one such democratic school close by, in Wheat Ridge, Colorado. I called them to ask if we, the Aspen Community School, could visit for a day. An adult answered and said that he would ask the students. A day later he called back and said, "The students say it's OK to come and visit, but they don't want any questions." I bought their book *Free at Last*, and our Community School students read it to one other.

Our traditional schools keep children "in our adult care" until the adults judge that they have the skills, knowledge, and maturity to take care of themselves. The tradition of this adult care is surveillance, control, and instruction; we justify this as protecting them from their immature selves. When we turn over important parts of their lives to them, such as justice, in an open-ended and continuous learning process, they choose to be mature about it. Do unto others … their turn in the dock might be next.

> *"'Why,' said the Dodo, 'the best way*
> *to explain it is to do it.'"*

> —Lewis Carroll

It doesn't happen often, but it really pricks up my ears when I hear, "I remember when you told me … "

A couple of days ago it was my old-time, ever-the-hippy teacher colleague Randi who filled it in with " … First, do no harm." This remark came within days of my starting to read Kirsten Olson's book *Wounded by School* and shortly after a physicist colleague told me, "For teachers to get respect they have to make firm and strong demands on the students."

My instant and angry response was "I *am* a respected teacher and I *never* make demands on my students." Just as well we dropped the subject, as I was embarrassed at my outburst. I do know that I don't make demands upon the students, and I don't much understand or want respect. What I think comes closer to describing a valued relationship between student and teacher is "I take you seriously because you take me seriously."

Is the dream of a school that does not wound utopian? Olson suggests, "A central function of the structure of education in America is preparation for a capitalistic society in which some will be winners and many will be losers. This means school *inevitably* involves sorting, tracking, and the scaffolding of human expectations, or, in essence, that wounding is necessary." Wow! Wounding is necessary? Ah, only if education remains the tool of a capitalistic military-industrial complex. I think we can, again, build a movement that says we will not send our children to schools that serve a society that demands that our schools wound our children. We will have to build different schools.

Olson's book is a well-told recounting of her extensive observations and interviews, but in focusing on the darkness of the wounded, does she do injustice to a whole public school system that also has its joys and triumphs? No, she speaks truth, and the truth is that there are too many wounded, it's unnecessary, and we know better. Our school system grew up in a struggle to indoctrinate immigrants, civilize rural life, and provide labor to an industrial and military society. In such a struggle it was inevitable and accepted that there would be wounded. We are in a new century with a school system from an old century, and the current level of the wounded is neither inevitable nor acceptable.

There is a minitheory of social action: When the public winces at the sight of excessive pain, a movement is born. Gandhi's salt march, King's marches from Selma to Montgomery, Mai Lai, and the endless body counts from Vietnam are oft-offered evidence. The notion of making schools better is as old as schools themselves. The recent failures to do so can be explained by the size of the enterprise and the attached blowflies of the establishment, which make change incredibly difficult. Indeed, we have a military-industrial-public school complex to deal with. Only a movement will change this. It's not the vision of better schools that will drive the movement, but instead an unwillingness to continue to inflict unnecessary and unjust pain. Olson's book, in which children tell their stories, is a necessary beginning.

I thought it important that our little Community School in Woody Creek, Colorado, maintain relationships and exchanges with other schools we could identify as progressive and child-centered. I remember a visit that Sydney Gurewitz Clemens paid to our campus. She ran a preschool in San Francisco and gave me her self-published book *The Sun's Not Broken, a Cloud's Just in the Way*, a recounting of children and events in classrooms committed to "First, do no harm." We chatted about how in a whole school committed to prioritizing damage control, staff supported each other, particularly when a teacher was having a bad moment. It seems to me that teachers generally avoid being critical of each other. Clemens said that her school had an agreement that if a teacher sees another teacher having difficulty he or she is asked, "Are you doing what you mean to be doing? If not, I am willing to take over for a while." I mentioned this at our next faculty meeting, and everyone said, "Yeah, yeah, a good idea," but it never took hold. I let it be.

Compulsory education doesn't have to make itself attractive in order to attract its consumers, the students, away from other activities, and evidently it hasn't. It does, however, have to present itself as valuable to the political structures that provide the public funding. It has made the case in economic terms: "Fund our compulsory education and we will deliver you both innovators and graduates who work hard and do what they are told." Somehow the same curriculum can deliver both of these. Neither teachers, students, nor child development experts were at the table for this deal, and thus they still play a minimal role in determining what school is all about.

No Child Left Behind makes schools accountable primarily through standardized test scores and secondarily through graduation rates. Accountability for public funding needs to be objective, of course, and also thorough—rigorous, I would say. Unfortunately the deal-makers have chosen an accountability methodology that is quantitative—which does necessarily translate to "objective"—and cheap: machine-scoreable multiple-choice pencil-and-paper tests. The deal-makers, in an effort to make the cheapest possible data look like accountability, mix it with demographic and financial data and call it "quantitative analysis that is data-based accountability."

Since students learn what they do, I suggest it would also be useful to report, objectively, an account of what students do.

"There are three kinds of lies:
lies, damned lies and statistics."

—Mark Twain

Well, I've scouted out some quantitative data that give some indicators about what students do.

From "Charting the Path from Engagement to Achievement: A Report on the 2009 High School Survey of Student Engagement," by Ethan Yazzie-Mintz:

> Two out of three respondents (66%) in 2009 are bored at least every day in class in high school; ... and approximately one out of every six students (17%) are bored in every class. Only 2% report never being bored ... more than four out of five noted a reason for their boredom as "material wasn't interesting" and about two out of five students claimed that the lack of relevance of the material caused their boredom ... one third of the students were bored because the "work wasn't challenging enough" ... 35% were bored due to "No interaction with teacher."

> Forty-nine percent reported giving their maximum effort in "most" or "all" of their classes. Nine percent of students reported giving their maximum effort in "none" of their classes, while 42% responded that they give their maximum effort in "1 or 2" of their classes.

> Students reported that their school contributed "Very Much" to their growth in the following areas: "Acquiring skills related to work after high school" (26%); "Writing effectively" (35%); "Speaking effectively" (30%);

"Reading and understanding challenging materials" (32%); "Learning independently" (32%); and "Solving real-world problems" (23%)."

From Janis N. Parham and Stephen P. Gordon's *Kappan* Volume 92, Number 5 article, "Moonlighting: A Harsh Reality for Many Teachers":

A more recent North Carolina survey found that 72% of the state's teachers had second jobs ... The No. 1 reason is financial need ... 67% of teachers surveyed believed that moonlighting had a negative effect on teaching performance.

Moonlighting helped the teachers develop a more positive attitude about themselves by helping them realize they could be successful at something other than teaching. The teachers reported that supervisors and clients at their moonlighting jobs gave them more respect than they got at their schools ...

Four out of five teachers said moonlighting led them to consider a new career ... A reason for rethinking their careers was that their moonlighting jobs had shown them there was a world of work beyond teaching, and one that would give them opportunities and rewards that teaching did not.

From an *American School Board Journal* Volume 198, Number 2 "School Law" article by Edwin C. Darden:

A survey by *Who's Who Among American High School Students* demonstrates that cheating is not isolated to students who struggle academically. The organization concluded that 76 percent of high-achieving teens cheated because it "didn't seem like a big deal." Even more disturbing is that students are accomplished cheaters. More than 90 percent of respondents said they had never been caught.

A Rutgers Management Education Center survey of 4,500 high school students discovered similarly that 75 percent of students participated in serious cheating, and 88 percent felt that cheating was "common" among their classmates.

We all agree that the classroom is where education happens, and I believe this accounting of the classroom should occupy more space in our national dialogue. I am sickened by front-page reports headlined "Student Achievement Improves Dramatically" that show last year's average score as 849 and this year's as 856, a less than 1 percent increase, probably less than the error bars that aren't reported, and taken in isolation rather than from a five- or ten-year trend.

"What we have to learn to do we learn by doing."

—ARISTOTLE

*"The purpose of education … is to create in
a person the ability to look at the world for
himself, to make his own decisions."*

—JAMES BALDWIN

Everybody says that teachers are the most important factor in students' learning and standardized test scores. Linda Darling-Hammond notes in her article "Evaluating Teacher Effectiveness" for the Center for American Progress, "Every aspect of school reform depends upon highly skilled teachers for its success. This is especially true as educational standards rise and the diversity of the student body increases. Teachers need even more sophisticated abilities to teach more complex curriculum to the growing number of public school students who have fewer educational resources at home, those who are new English language learners, and those who have distinctive learning needs."

But if teachers have tremendous power to mold children into thoughtful and effective adults who participate actively in the economy and community, it follows that they have the power to mold children in ways that are outside of our desires or social norms, too. The Jesuit motto as they go about conversion is, "Give me the child until he is seven and I will give you the man," which is just a frank statement about the ease of brainwashing the young.

OK, there's a great deal at stake. Schools can not only brainwash our children, they can change the political structure of the government; can we give them that much power without proper oversight? No parent or nation should ignore this. The classroom core has evolved to make this oversight difficult; what goes on between teachers and students goes on behind closed doors. Are we simply to trust that these teachers are good and that they are brainwashing our kids to the best social norms of our community?

Consequently there are controls and surveillance. Principals do classroom observations, but how do we know we can trust the principals? We adopt standards of what is to be taught, and the standards are more than can be, or should be, either taught or learned. In this regime there is no brainwashing or sedition because there is no time left for that. A consequence is, however, that teachers do not feel trusted in their work. They feel overworked, underpaid, and doubted, not a great recipe for attracting our best and brightest into the field.

The McKinsey report "Closing the Talent Gap: Attracting and Retaining Top-Third Graduates to Careers in Teaching" notes, "Most students see teaching as unattractive in terms of quality of the people in the field, professional growth and compensation." Currently schools of education enroll students from the bottom one-third of SAT scores.

"Classroom teaching is perhaps the most complex,
most challenging, and most demanding,
subtle, nuanced, and frightening activity
that our species has ever invented."

—LEE SHULMAN

The education magazine *Kappan*, Volume 92, Number 4 carries this gritty title: "Pressuring Teachers to Leave: Honest Talk about How Principals Use Harassing Supervision." The lead story reads, "After 23 years in Room 101, across from the main office, Mrs. Albany returns to start a new school year to find that she has been assigned to room 411, four flights up in a building with an elevator that seldom works. Climbing stairs is difficult for Mrs. Albany, and her schedule requires that she walk up the stairs several times throughout the day … Rather than relying on the district's formal dismissal procedure, the principal used an alternative method to pressure teachers perceived to be of low quality, and it worked."

Well, sort of worked; she didn't leave teaching, she just went on down the road and into another school. "In a study of Chicago principals conducted in 2008-09, 37 of the 40 principals who were interviewed described engaging in harassing supervision." Most principals expressed regret at their own actions, but said it was in the students' best interests, and therefore justified. It's the best that can done, given the "system's dysfunctions."

Let me pick out another piece from the jumbled pile of puzzle pieces that is the American public education system. Charles M. Payne, in *So Much Reform: So Little Change*, writes of his extensive and deeply personal involvement in school reform, particularly in Chicago:

> We have not learned from all this experimentation nearly as much as
> we might have. Much of this experience has just been wasted. From

individual schools to school districts, to the research community itself, the entities responsible for the management and analysis of urban schools are themselves constructed in such a way as to make it very difficult for them to learn from their own experiences … At the school level, the district level, and the national level, even where we see some progress, we continue to see attempts to implement reform in ways that are manifestly unlikely to work. Some of this is just political expediency or earnest incompetence, but some of it is that people in leadership positions do not have a systemic understanding of the causes of failure, in part because the same dysfunctional social arrangements that do so much to cause failure also do a great deal to obscure its origins. The process mystifies itself.

And now back to the aforementioned *Kappan* article, which closes with: "Harassing supervision makes it clear that reforming schools is as much changing the nature of schools as workplaces for adults as it is about improving schools as institutions of learning for children. And perhaps the two are not unrelated."

"Knowing is a process, not a product."

—JEROME BRUNER

"Neither teachers or students can be trusted to make any important decisions about their lives in school." Bruce Thomas wrote this; I've been carrying it around with me now for twenty years, as the teacher in me finds it both true and maddening.

Trust, *n*. Reliance on the integrity, strength, ability, surety, etc., of a person or thing; confidence.

—*syn*. Certainty, belief, faith. TRUST, ASSURANCE, CONFIDENCE imply a feeling of security. TRUST implies instinctive, unquestioning belief in and reliance upon something. CONFIDENCE implies conscious trust because of good reasons, definite evidence, or past experience. ASSURANCE implies absolute confidence and certainty.

The "lack of assurance" part is out there in plain sight: "Here are the standards to which you will teach and here are the assessments to prove that you did so." Less visible, but certainly felt, is society's lack of "instinctive, unquestioning belief in and reliance upon" its teachers. It makes it difficult for us to trust back, and that has consequences in our classrooms.

The alarming miracle of Google and the Internet is the delivery, on October 23, 2010, of the October 21, 2010 decision by the United States Court of Appeals, Sixth Circuit, in the case of *Shelley Evans-Marshall v. Board of Education of the Tipp City Exempted Village School District* to resolve the question "Does a public high school teacher have a First (and Fourteenth) Amendment right to 'select books and methods of instruction for use in the classroom without interference from public officials'?"

(The Fourteenth Amendment includes the "equal protection of the laws" phrase, which was the basis of the *Brown v. Board of Education* decision.) Summary: English teacher uses Hermann Hesse's *Siddhartha* in her curriculum. The school board had authorized its purchase several years before. Some parents object to the book on the basis of "decency and excellence in the classroom." Principal and teacher argue over things, and teacher gets her first negative evaluation, which she appeals to the superintendent. The school board votes unanimously not to rehire teacher "due to problems with communication and teamwork." Teacher files First Amendment lawsuit in 2003. OK, it takes seven years for a decision, but the wheels of justice grind slowly.

The ruling states, "In the light cast by *Garcetti*, it is clear that the First Amendment does not generally insulate Evans-Marshall from employer discipline, even discipline prompted by her curricular and pedagogical choices and even if it otherwise appears that the school administrators treated her shabbily. When a teacher teaches, the school system does not regulate that speech as much as it hires that speech. Expression is a teacher's stock in trade, the commodity she sells to her employer in exchange for a salary. And if it is the school board that hires the speech, it can surely regulate the content of what is or is not expressed, what is expressed, in other words, on its behalf."

The court added this "don't be such a nuisance again" warning: "When educators disagree over what should be assigned, as is surely bound to happen if each of them has a First Amendment right to influence the curriculum, whose free-speech rights win? Placing the First Amendment's stamp of approval on these kinds of debates not only would demand permanent judicial intervention in the conduct of governmental operations, but it also would transform run-of-mine curricular disputes into constitutional stalemates."

And finally, "Ohio law gives elected officials—the school board—not teachers, not the chair of a department, not the principal, not even the superintendent, responsibility over the curriculum. This is an accountability measure, pure and simple, one that assures the citizens of a community have a say over a matter of considerable importance to many of them—their children's education—by giving them control over membership on the board." In other words, you teachers and education administrators are not trusted with even the curriculum. Has anybody ever seen a school board where a majority were educators?

Could this mistrust possibly be related to our difficulty, unlike some other nations, to recruit our best and brightest to become teachers?

"The people must get to the mountain.
Doors must open and close.
How to savor the savagery of Egyptians,
Who betrayed the names of their gods
To demons, and tore the hair
From their godheads
And lotus blossoms are pulled out of the pool."

—Harvey Shapiro

By the time we get past tea and crumpets and to the fifth definition for the verb to *serve*, we find, "to render assistance; be of use; help." Down at the bottom, after definition thirty-three about tennis, we find the verb originates from the Latin *servire*, equivalent to *serv(us)*, slave. Most of us, teachers included, in the so-called helping professions use the fifth definition and endow it with voluntariness; we serve by choice, and as such we have a certain freedom to do it our own way, which is understood and agreed upon by both the served and the server.

The agreement largely disappears with the word "servant," "a person in the service of another." A servant is an employee employed by an employer and does what he or she is told, thus there is very little bargaining. The arrangement can be terminated by either party.

The same Latin root serves, too, for "servitude," "Slavery or bondage of any kind." It is pretty much being a servant, only you can't just up and quit. The aspiring teacher hopes to serve, but once in a classroom finds herself a servant. And if teachers don't quit, as 50 percent do by their fifth year, it becomes servitude, as the employment world out there offers no attractive jobs to worn-out teachers.

For students, since school is compulsory, we can refer directly to the word "slave." I freely describe the classroom situation as oppressive, *adj.* 1. Burdensome, unjustly harsh, or tyrannical. 2. Causing discomfort by being excessive, intense, elaborate, etc. 3. Distressing or grievous for both teacher and students. The characteristics of an oppressor-oppressed system include:

- The oppressed have an "underground" system of communication that allows them to talk about the oppression among themselves.
- The oppressors have ways that limit their accessibility to the oppressed. The oppressed can easily be dismissed from their presence.
- Oppressors have more rights and freedoms in the given organization than the oppressed.
- Oppressors have regulatory powers over the oppressed; they are "top dogs" and have dominance.

- The oppressor has a rational argument, based on a belief system, that the oppressed either deserve oppression or are inferior in some way, which supports the "goodness" of their oppression.
- The oppressed have less activity in the various economies of the organization. They are "poor."
- The oppressed are denied outside investment in their economies.
- The oppressed have an acceptance culture about their oppression. Their struggle for identity and meaning can be found in the rituals, practices, and content of their culture.
- The oppressed often describe spiritual rewards that compensate for their material situation.

If a system displays these characteristics, is it oppressive?

"The slave can hardly escape deluding himself into thinking that he is choosing to obey his master's commands when, in fact, he is obliged to."

—W. H. Auden

Frederick Douglass writes in a 1849 letter to an abolitionist associate:

Let me give you a word on the philosophy of reform. The whole history of the progress of human liberty shows that all concessions yet made to her august claims have been born of earnest struggle. The conflict has been exciting, agitating, all absorbing, and for the time being putting all other tumults to silence. It must do this or it does nothing. If there is no struggle there is no progress. Those who profess to favor freedom, and yet deprecate agitation, are men who want crops without plowing up the ground. They want rain without thunder and lightning. They want the ocean without the awful roar of its many waters. This struggle may be a moral one; or it may be a physical one; or it may be both moral and physical; but it must be a struggle. Power concedes nothing without a demand. It never did and it never will. Find out just what people will submit to, and you have found the exact amount of injustice and wrong which will be imposed upon them; and these will continue until they are resisted with either words or blows, or with both. The limits of tyrants are prescribed by the endurance of those whom they oppress.

Our public school system is not going to easily let the inmates take over.

"If the kids are learning in the streets,
let's change the nature of the street and
let's change the nature of learning."

—Barbara Mikulski

Liz, with over twenty years' experience in the classroom, and I were managing a residential program to train teachers, guys and gals who had obtained a degree in something other than teaching, mature folks deciding to become teachers. Observing our adult acolytes in a residential program ensured that we knew their characters and personalities. Whether for adults or for the young, teaching is filled with complexities, uncertainties, surprises, and resistance. Talking through some of these, I mentioned to Liz, "'Teacher' is a beautiful word." "Oh," said Liz with surprise, "I'd never thought of it that way." Her surprise gave me pause; she's right, in common usage "teacher" is not a beautiful word.

I recalled the saying "Those who can, do; those who can't, teach."

What I think I really meant was, "Liz, you and I are trying to teach these young adults to be beautiful teachers, no matter the common usage of the word 'teacher.'"

When I am introduced as an educator, I correct the person introducing me: "I am a teacher," I say.

Teacher, *n*. A person who teaches or instructs.

Teach, *v*. 3. To impart knowledge or skill; give instruction.

—*syn*. Inform, enlighten, discipline, drill, school, indoctrinate. TEACH, INSTRUCT, TUTOR, TRAIN, EDUCATE, share the meaning of imparting information, understanding, or skill. TEACH is the broadest and most general of these terms and can refer to almost any practice that causes others to develop skill or knowledge.

When I am in a classroom, in a school and with people much younger than I, it is clear to all that I am distinct from the rest, I am *the teacher*. I *belong* in this setting in a different way than the rest; in fact, I feel separate from the rest. This puts me on edge and leads eventually to my thinking of "teacher" as "community organizer within a democratic classroom."

Shepherd, *n*. 2. A person who protects, guides, or watches over a person or group of people.

Janie was a seasoned third-grade teacher and used time-outs to discipline in order to ensure classroom control. I debated with her about the usefulness of removing a student from the class, even if temporarily. She agreed with me that it was a punishment, an infliction of some pain, that one consequence was anger and resentment from the student, and that it was often the same student, time after time. Time-outs didn't make any fundamental change, I argued, therefore they weren't a learning experience. Then she said, "It's not what you do, it's how you do it."

I hung around long enough to get a look-see at how she did it. It was Sam whose behavior prompted the intervention. Janie dropped to her knees so that her face was even with Sam's; she looked deep into his eyes and gently grasped his hands. "Sam,

honey, I know you can't help it, but I'm going to ask you to take a time-out for five minutes and for you to think about it while you're gone." Indeed, it's not what you do, it's how you do it. The *it* that Sam was sent to think about was left entirely up to him.

> Minister, *v.* 9. To give service, care, or aid; attend, as to wants or necessities.

Deborah Meier said this, "Teaching is mostly listening, and learning is mostly telling." Indeed, it's how you do it.

> Nurse, *v.* 9. To look after carefully so as to promote growth, development, etc.; foster, cherish.

Reuben got sent to the principal's office about the twentieth time he disappeared from his third/fourth-grade classroom without telling anyone. He answered his teacher's questions, "Why? Is something wrong?" with a shrug. We talked of many things about his life both in and outside of school before we closed in on his specific escapist behavior. "My dad says I have to stand up and fight anyone who treats me with disrespect, particularly if it's about me being a Jew. If the kids tease me at all, I think I'm supposed to fight. I don't want to fight, so I run away and hide." I explained to him that while he should listen to and try to understand his dad's instructions, things were different in our school. He was right not to fight; here we talked things through, even when it was difficult; teachers were here to help with this. He was ready to return to class after three hours.

> *"A teacher teaches individuals, not classes. A teacher*
> *sees the possibilities in her students. A teacher gives*
> *hope. A teacher gives voice. A teacher navigates.*
> *A teacher explores. A teacher is patient. A teacher*
> *learns with his or her students. A teacher discovers.*
> *A teacher is a parent. A teacher accepts children as*
> *they are, not as he or she would like them to be."*
>
> —Bernard Gassaway

And a teacher is on edge.

*"Teachers seem lonely; they fight battles alone with
their consciences and, it seems, frequently lose."*

—DAN LORTIE

*"The self is not ready-made, but something in
continuous formation through choice of action."*

—JOHN DEWEY

We who engaged with the alternative schools movement of the seventies did so out of anger, anger at an educational system that was complicit with a military-industrial complex that was satisfied with centuries of segregation and that engaged in an illegal war that was killing civilians.

We would not, could not, send our children to these schools. We didn't know how to march against the educational system, so we simply started our own schools. It was easy for us to toss around the words "open," "free," "democratic," "community," and "child-centered." But after you've gathered the children into a place with untrained and uncertified teachers, there's a real question: "What do I do Monday?" Soon we found ourselves reading John Holt's book of that title, and Neil Postman, George Dennison, Jonathan Kozol, and many others to discover that we were all reinventing the progressive education of John Dewey, Francis Parker, Jane Addams, and others.

"Progressive educators believed that a new education program, based on the development of cooperative social skills, critical thinking and democratic behaviors, could play a pivotal role in transforming a society of greed, individualism, waste and corruption for one based on compassion, humanism and equality," wrote S. Alexander Rippa in *Education in a Free Society: An American History*. What or who remained of this previous effort? Could we join together their earlier experience and our current energy? There had been the Progressive Education Association formed in 1919, which was the author of the important but largely forgotten "Eight-Year Study" of the 1930s and 1940s. Was the association still around? In the mid-nineties I tracked the PEA down to a street address in Pasadena; my mail was returned, addressee unknown. They had formally folded in 1955, and by the nineties there was no one left.

No problem, we thought, it's time to start a new association. A dozen of us self-selected and met on the campus of the University of California at Santa Cruz to create the Alliance of Progressive Educators. Martin Tadlock came from the graduate school of education at Utah State University. When his turn came, he told this story about his democratic classroom:

> It's the students' first-year required course in education. They come in the first day and we sit around a large round table. I have a flip chart behind me. After a while one of them says, "Professor T, when are we going to start?" And I say, "What do you want me to do?" "Teach us," they say, and I say, "The course is called The Democratic Classroom, and it is run as a democratic classroom so that you learn by doing. What do you want to learn?" They answer, "To learn how to teach," and I answer, "Let's make a list of what that would look like, you guys tell me, I'll write on the flip chart," and they start throwing out ideas of what they need to know in order to know how to teach.

We ask Martin how good is the students' list. He says, "Darn good, if it's weak at all, it's weak on the history and philosophy of education. If that happens, I have some tricks for getting them to fix it." He then describes how the students go about prioritizing and time-ordering the list, and how students volunteer to find what books would be useful for their purpose. And so it goes for the year—a democratic classroom.

The young lady who accompanies Martin speaks during her turn: "I took Professor T's class and now I teach a democratic fifth and sixth–grade classroom the way he taught us. There are two of us, and we have eighty kids in the class." Wow, this is not theory, this is a battlefield exercise! "It goes quite well," she says. "They know quite precisely what they need to know and do to be ready for seventh grade. I fill in the few gaps and give some help in choosing materials."

I like very much this leveling of the power relationship between teacher and students. She and Martin are describing operationally what I have been calling "teacher as community organizer, teaching as community organizing." I ask, "As the students learn that they are in charge of their own curriculum, do they also learn to take charge of behavior problems, or do they still expect you to be the enforcer, the cop?" "Yes," she says. "It's noisy for a while, but when they realize that I am not willing to be their cop, they begin to take over that job too."

Never do for others what they can do for themselves. Never. The iron, or golden, rule of community organizing.

Martin came and did a workshop for us at the Aspen Community School, and we had an Alliance meeting a year later. That was the last meeting, and there were nice but not democratic classrooms at our school. It is hard for me to accept how much we accept nowadays.

> *"Taking responsibility for one's own education should
> not be confused with taking courses."*
>
> —Seymour Sarason

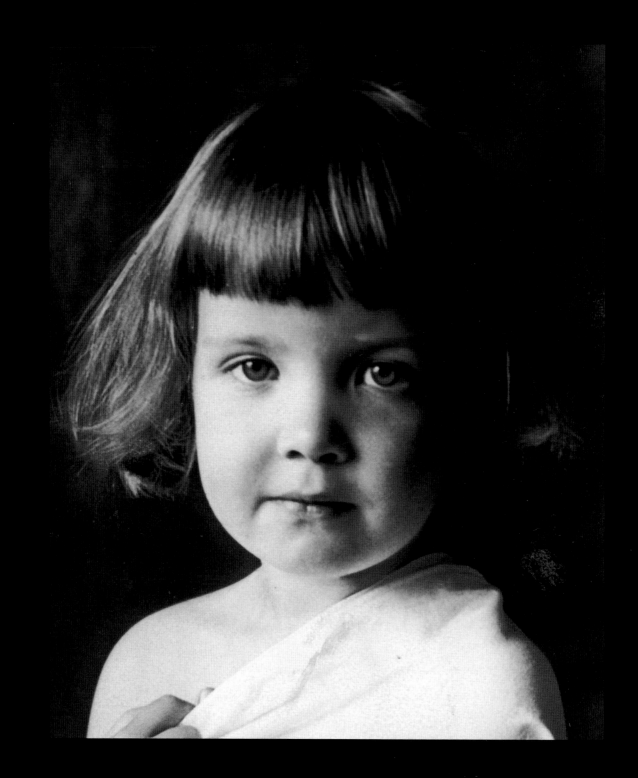

A community is a group of agents, people, or institutions that have commonality. The folks who live in a neighborhood are a community; those working in a factory or an industry are a community; those who live in wheelchairs are a community; a classroom is a community. The churches and/or schools of a neighborhood are a community of institutions. Organizing is the activity of putting the parts of a community—its members—into a state of coherence and action toward a common vision.

In common usage, "community organizing" implies a purpose of making things better for the community involved, i.e., there is a cause. The process involves defining and building a membership, defining and adopting the cause, understanding the mechanics of creating change, and then implementation. My friend Frank Sanchez has spent a life in community organizing, and I asked him once for a definition. He said that he liked to explain it this way:

- Good community organizing wins immediate and concrete improvement in people's lives.
- Good community organizing gives people a sense of their own power.
- Good community organizing alters the relationships of power.
- Good community organizing springs from the concerns of the common interest.
- Good community organizing understands individual wants.
- Good community organizing is based on relationships and self-interests.
- Good community organizing develops leadership.
- Good community organizing implements collective ways of solving problems.
- Good community organizing both confronts and negotiates.
- Good community organizing teaches about democracy and creative conflict.

- Good community organizing provides a critical social analysis.
- Good community organizing brings about imagination and dreams of the possible.
- Good community organizing produces public judgment through public dialogue.
- Good community organizing includes appreciation, celebration, evaluation, and reflection.
- Good community organizing trains mentors.
- Good community organizing supports and sustains personal transformation.
- Good community organizing creates a learning community.

It's about coming together—together we are more than we are separately—to bring about changes that benefit all of us. The status quo is going to be changed for our benefit, and it takes power to move the status quo. Community organizing creates that power, people power.

I found in South Texas a group of parents angry that there were no soap dishes in the school bathrooms. They organized, went to the school board en masse, and got the soap dishes. With this immediate and concrete improvement in their children's lives, they went on to get effective school programs and eventually became players in the Texas Industrial Areas Foundation Alliance schools.

A community organization usually begins with a few activists, the moms outraged about the soap dishes, for example. If the community is indeed ready and charged enough to become organized, the movement grows; "There's more to fix in our schools than soap dishes," they say, and soon enough there are more members and activities than a few volunteer activists can manage. It takes someone with the knowledge, skills, and time to be the community organizer, and that person needs to be paid for his or her time and expertise. The organizer is not a leader; a leader is the one who tells the story and/or leads the life that the community aspires to. In community organizing lingo, a leader is one who has followers. The organizer, on the other hand, builds relationships within the community, arranges meetings, holds members accountable, develops leadership among the members, and generally knows the established tricks of the trade by which the community becomes organized.

Saul Alinsky is more or less the acknowledged father of American community organizing, founding the church-based Industrial Areas Foundation to deal with oppression in Chicago's Back of the Yards neighborhood. Someone asked him, "What is a community organizer?" With only a moment's thought he replied, "A great teacher." If Alinsky can say that a community organizer is a great teacher, then within the structure of education can't we say a great teacher is a community organizer? When, as a classroom teacher, I look at the Sanchez list, I declare those to be exactly my learning goals for this little community, my class. Exactly. Most teachers who have a great class and a great year don't brag about test scores but about the solid relationships built upon commonality and the development of leadership among the students.

I made a little PR campaign about "teaching as community organizing, teacher as community organizer" and paraded it around a few educational forums, collecting very few followers. Thinking a little more about that, I realize that the education world is aflood with great new ideas and techniques for teachers, and one more is just one more. Understanding community organizing as empowerment and as capable of examining the established relationships of power within schools and altering the relationships of power, I see the tensions. Compulsory schooling is organized around divide-and-conquer power relationships. Organized classrooms are not just an educational technique, they are also a subversion and a revolution against the existing power structures. Few teachers are left with the energy at the end of the school day to start revolutions.

Tom Gaudet, an organizer and son of an organizer, said at one of our workshops, "Teachers cannot self-organize, they need an outside organizer in order to organize." That was the moment our superintendent tipped over his chair and stormed out. "We have our procedures for a teacher to express a grievance, and we expect teachers to follow those procedures," he said.

"Not only education for democracy,
but education as democracy."

—B. Glickman

A teacher plays a vital role in the classroom, enough so that he is usually the only person in the room to carry that title. The word "teacher" has many meanings, precisely because teaching is an extraordinarily complex job. If I had to pick one word alone to describe a good teacher, I would choose "organizer." "To organize" means "to form as or into a whole consisting of interdependent or coordinated parts, esp. for harmonious or united action." With twenty students in a class, what does it take to make a coordinated whole? Including the teacher there are 210 different pairwise interactions and 1,330 different three-party interactions, and so on; it's not just twenty independent teacher-to-student relationships, although these are particularly important and are included in the 210 pairwise interactions.

The teacher is responsible for authoring or creating the setting that is the classroom. "Creating a setting is one of man's most absorbing experiences, compounded as it is of dreams, hopes, effort and thought," wrote Seymour Sarason. All of the above interactions need to be accommodated in a good learning setting. The good teacher creates a setting that has sufficient complexity and yet is organized for "harmonious or united action." The good teacher understands that learning is a socially constructed activity, and thus understands the culture and sociology of the classroom, the school, and the neighborhood.

Born in Croatia, Mihaly "Iron Mike" Csikszentmihalyi wrote *Flow: The Psychology of Optimal Experience* in which he examined and popularized the word "flow" to describe the psychological state of energized focus, full involvement, and single-minded immersion. I chatted about third and fourth grade with Iron Mike when he was still at the University of Chicago; "Vee drag dem too zoon out of de mud," he said.

Csikszentmihalyi imagined a space where one dimension is the challenge presented by an activity and the other is the skill required for the activity. Flow is possible when the skills match the challenge and both are high, and the person is performing the activity for intrinsic purposes. When someone is in the flow state, he or she is completely engrossed with the one task at hand and, without making the conscious decision to do so, loses awareness of all other things: time, people, distractions, and even basic bodily needs. This occurs because all of the attention of the person in the flow state is on the task at hand; there is simply no more attention available to be allocated. Flow is a very positive feeling, and if the activity is teaching or learning it is the state of maximum teaching or learning.

Imagine a classroom setting where every student is intrinsically motivated to deeply engage in a learning activity that is at her highest limit of skill and challenge. The organizer of such a setting will certainly be at his highest limit of skill and challenge too. This is an extraordinarily complex system, and everything is set for the emergent phenomena of a group flow, the perfect classroom. Phrases like "classroom control," "differentiated instruction," or even "instruction" are useless to describe this utopian setting.

Richard F. Elmore is a sensible senior professor in the Harvard Graduate School of Education and wrote this in an ongoing "Futures of School Reform" blog for *Education Week* (May 16, 2011):

> I recently spent the better part of a week in a West Coast school district, working with its leadership team on their high school renewal initiative. We spent most of two days observing classrooms, talking in a structured way with teachers and administrators from the district about what they saw in the classrooms we visited, and talking generally about their plans for renewal of high schools. I spend a lot of time in classrooms like these, a lot of it in high schools. This was a particularly depressing visit, not because it was atypical, but because of how typical it is of what I routinely see in my visits. Consider the following two examples:

A "regular" (non-honors) English class. Thirty-six students are sitting in rows in a darkened classroom at 10:00 AM. The teacher is showing final minutes of a video on a 1950s classic high school text. As I scan the rows, I see four students asleep with earbuds in place. Six students in the middle facing the teacher are carrying on a conversation having nothing to do with the subject of the class over the top of the teacher's attempts to engage the class in a discussion. Four students sitting in the back are engaged in a valiant attempt to salvage the discussion by responding to the teacher's questions. The teacher calls on these four students repeatedly. The remainder of the class sits silently, staring into space, waiting for the bell to ring. An "honors" English class. Thirty-one students are sitting in rows in a brightly-lit classroom, each with a fat three-ring notebook. By their dress, their ease of interaction, their casual demeanor of privilege, it is clear these are the "chosen" students. The topic of discussion for the class is how to organize the notebook into a portfolio—which papers and quizzes go into which tabs, where to put teacher comments, what to do with class notes, etc. It is clear that the students are having a good time doing this; it is also clear that they have written a total of about ten pages of prose between January and May; and it is clear that the main reason they are having a good time is that they are forestalling whatever the "work" is for that day. After 45 minutes of excruciatingly detailed, rule-oriented discussion of what goes where in the portfolio, the teacher suggests that the students spend the next 40 minutes silently reading a section of the text.

I wish these were exceptional examples. They are not. I wish that the teachers and administrators who were observing classrooms with me were as outraged by what we saw as I was. They were not. They saw nothing exceptional or unusual about these classrooms. Mostly what I see in my visits to middle and upper grades classrooms are examples of what Michael Sedlack, et al. (1986), long-ago characterized as "the bargain"—"you give me order and attendance, I'll give you passing grades and [minimal] homework." The only other public institution in our society that works this way, with this degree of focus and dedication, is the prison system. At the extreme—in Advanced Placement classrooms, for example—teachers stress volume, coverage, pace, and recall, but these classrooms are exceptional only in the velocity of work, not in its focus on accommodation and control. For most students, the pace of work is like a thick sludge, moving in no particular direction toward a destination defined by escape. U.S. secondary schools, it seems, are primarily custodial institutions, designed to hold adolescents out of the labor force and to socialize them to adult control. Nothing particularly original in this observation.

As I read the collected entries in the "Futures of School Reform" blog, they seem bright, energetic, combative, and optimistic about the future of the enterprise of American public schooling. I wonder, as I read them, whether the writers are aware of what classrooms in American secondary schools actually look like—the dismal, glacial, adult-centered, congenially authoritative, mindless soup in which our children spend the bulk of their days. I wonder whether people are aware of how robust the old "bargain" is in the face of so-called high-stakes accountability; how little the monolithic beast of American secondary education has been affected by the bright, high-minded optimism of professional reformers; how little the exemplars that professional reformers use to justify their role in society have actually affected the lives of adolescents.

I wonder, finally, what would happen if we simply opened the doors and let the students go; if we let them walk out of the dim light of the overhead projector into the sunlight; if we let them decide how, or whether, to engage this monolith. Would it be so terrible? Could it be worse than what they are currently experiencing? Would adults look at young people differently if they had to confront their children on the street rather than locking them away in institutions? Would it force us to say more explicitly what a humane and healthy learning environment might look like? Should discussions of the future of school reform be less about the pet ideas of professional reformers and more about what we're doing to young people in the institution called school?

*"The sad fact is that most reformers don't
acknowledge the realities of classroom teaching,
where both God and the devil are in the details."*

—MARY M. KENNEDY

"Teaching is the most difficult profession of them all," educator Lee Shulman recently told a group of teachers and psychologists. "The only time a physician comes close to doing what a teacher does is when the doctor faces an emergency room of multiple patients with multiple conditions, all of whom need immediate attention. That's what a teacher deals with every day in a class of thirty," he noted.

Shulman described a few of the basics required of the expert teacher: cognitive understanding of how students learn; emotional preparation to relate to many students whose varied needs are not always evident; content knowledge from which to draw different ways to present a concept; and, finally, the ability to make teaching decisions quickly and act on them.

"And they are expected to do all this constantly, with a twenty-minute break for lunch," he added.

In his 2009 book *Why Don't Students Like School?*, cognitive scientist Daniel T. Willingham also upholds the complexity of teaching, explaining that teaching must be an "act of persuasion" if teachers are to convince students that learning is worth the effort. Although principles from cognitive science such as "Know your students" sometimes sound like bubbe psychology— that is, commonsense wisdom that your grandmother has always known—that doesn't make these principles easy to master, he writes. Both learning and teaching require practice.

Philip C. Rodkin in *Educational Leadership* describes, in utter impracticality, what teachers should do about bullying among students.

Survey students regularly on whether they are being harassed or have witnessed harassment. Make it easier for students to come to an adult in the school to talk about harassment by building staff-student relationships ... Know whom students hang out with, who their friends are, and whom they dislike. Know whom students perceive to be popular and unpopular. Connect with students who have no friends ... Identify student leaders who can encourage peers to stand against bullying. Assess whether student social norms are *really* against bullying ... Implement an intellectually challenging character education or socio-emotional learning curriculum. Teach students how to achieve their goals by being assertive rather than aggressive ...

I walked down the hall past two footballers who had cornered a known nerd. He looked terrified, but didn't ask for help. I had only two minutes before my next class and really needed a cup of coffee and a moment of rest in the teachers' lounge. I strode by without eye contact.

"Every early elementary school classroom is full
of embryonic criminals. It's as natural for little kids
to lie and steal as it is for them to breathe. They
cheat, fight, show disrespect, and harass each
other sexually as free of guilt as if they had just
eaten a hot dog. Until intervention. The only
question becomes, then, what style?"

—Eliot Wigginton

A Predicament of Innocents

He was spoken to, or about, always as E. J. Kapella, and the high school kids talked about him quite a lot. E. J. Kapella taught drivers' ed and shop; drivers' ed brought him into contact with essentially all of the students, and they all trash-talked him, to his face, to each other.

You know high schools; you would be a queer if you didn't go along with the crowd. It was mostly the guys who took shop as a gut. There was a woodstove in the shop both for heat and to get rid of scraps and sawdust. Doug told me how he shoved in a carton of 9mm Luger shells and how, as they popped off, E. J. Kapella pretended it wasn't happening. As near as I could tell, E. J. Kapella interpreted all of the attention as, "Heck, the reason they joke around is because they kind of like me."

David Jones was also well known and talked about, and like E. J. Kapella, was always referred to by his full name, David Jones. I met him his senior year in my physics class. He carried a briefcase and never took off his felt porkpie hat. Because my course was based upon passing tests rather than class attendance and David Jones was good at passing tests, I didn't see him often. Whenever we did meet he talked quietly and hurriedly about stuff like quarks and black holes. His dad would call me some evenings to tell me how bright his son was: "He's nearly finished with an alternative theory of relativity." His classmates did not regard him as just another nerd; he was the school's unique nerdiest of all nerds and was treated as an untouchable alien.

One day, after he had given me a little review of his work on superconductivity, he told me, "There is one teacher here who has made all the difference in my life, E. J. Kapella." I have since been more cautious about judging either teachers or students by any simple measures. You just never know …

"Teachers are to schools as gardeners are to gardens—
tenders not only of the plants but of the
soil in which they grow."

—John I. Goodlad

Claire lived in our neighborhood, went to the same high school attended by my two eldest and where I taught. She would drop over, oh, maybe three or four times a month, have a beer or two, and just talk. Sometimes she brought her little brother Timmie; they both said, "To get away from our parents for a while."

I had come to the habit of listening without judgment or much comment to folks older or younger than I. This, a successful strategy as a child, I found useful as a parent and as a teacher. Let them tell their story; an occasional "humph" or "I'll be darned" served as acknowledgement and encouragement to continue.

Doc Farner, too, lived in our neighborhood. We adults knew little about her circumstances, but the kids, Claire included, knew it all. She had lost her license to practice medicine and lived with her daughter, Beth, and a teenage son, Eric, who shot up junk and slept under the pool table in the basement. One night Claire said she had recently been to Doc Farner's. The doctor had hooked up a warm saline IV directly into her femoral artery. "What a sex rush," she said.

Thirty-five years later Claire sent a note of condolence over Hunter Thompson's death, ending with, "You have no idea what it meant, and still means now, that you thought I was a person worth listening to."

This week, now forty years later, I got a long letter. She is poor, bipolar, living with her wife, and painting beautiful covers for a lesbian magazine. The handwriting is difficult to read, but closes with, "I think you're one of the 1st adult males who was safe. You helped by just being and created an enduring flame of peace, love and gratitude. P.S. Beth Farner and I have reconnected."

Being a listener is not without its dilemmas and predicaments. You won't hear anything but polite banter unless they believe you won't rat them out or go all righteous on them. And if you are safe, you are going to hear things like what went on at Doc Farner's. Part of the agreement is that I won't tell anybody unless directed to. As a listener in what is now a fairly intimate relationship, I am obliged to think through my moral responsibilities. In this case, the saline IV. I said, "That's far out.

Are you OK with it?" "Sure," she said, and I felt that I had done all that was needed to be done at that time. And yet, even now, I look back on other options that I had and feel doubts. I'm still not comfortable with the ending, but then this listening business is simply more important than being comfortable.

Afterword: Claire and I have been exchanging notes and art for a year now. This came yesterday: "We're waiting for the autopsy to be 100% certain, my sister Sara was found in her apartment deceased. No one knows exactly when she made her transition; again, we're waiting for that info too. It's sad, she burned her bridges and used alcohol and pain killers to the point recovery was beside the point. She was crazy/ upside down and extremely manipulative. I wanted you to know George, she liked you a lot. With sorrow, Claire."

My youngest sister died during one of my years of tenure as principal at the Community School. There had been multiple trips over to Boulder and the sharing with siblings of this process. Everyone in the school knew what was going on and gave me room to be elsewhere as much as I needed to be. One lunch hour the receptionist, Sue, told me softly, "They just called to say that she died a few minutes ago." No surprise of course, but a great leaden feeling dropped over me and I said, "I'm going home now for awhile." Next day, plans were falling into place for the memorial: date and place, and that I would be the officiate—this is difficult stuff; I yearned to grieve in remote silence. I was standing at the bottom of the steps to the stage and young Jonathan, third grade, climbed up three steps above, where he could reach his arm across my shoulders. "Are you OK?" he asked. Surprised and concerned about what response I might find that would be that teachable moment for him I simply said, "Yeah." "Go softly," he said, and I realized he had found the teachable moment for me.

My progressive-education-savvy friend Bruce Thomas alerted me to Louis P. Benezet, who in 1929 was the superintendent of schools in Manchester, New Hampshire. As usual, an alert from Bruce was worth tracking down; both Google and Wiki worked, and I found the three papers he wrote in 1935 in the *Journal of the National Education Association*. He writes in informal narrative, and it's a good read. Here I've chosen a few highlights:

> It seems to me that we waste much time in the elementary schools, wrestling with stuff that ought to be omitted or postponed until the children are in need of studying it. If I had my way, I would omit arithmetic from the first six grades ... I feel that it is all nonsense to take eight years to get children thru the ordinary arithmetic assignment of the elementary schools. What possible needs has a ten-year-old child for a knowledge of long division? The whole subject of arithmetic could be postponed until the seventh year of school, and it could be mastered in two years' study by any normal child.

And this he did with a sample of classrooms within his district, "to try the experiment of abandoning all formal instruction in arithmetic below the seventh grade and concentrating on teaching to read, to reason, and to recite—my new Three Rs. And by reciting I did not mean giving back, verbatim, the words of the teacher or of the textbook. I meant speaking the English language."

Of course, Benezet experienced plenty of opposition from parents, school boards, principals, and teachers, and much of his papers' content is about the experiments he performed to establish different student outcomes between his experimental classrooms and traditional classrooms. He did not use scores from standardized machine-gradable questions. Here's one sample problem: "The distance from Boston to Portland by water is 120 miles. Three steamers left from Boston, simultaneously, for Portland. One makes the trip in 10 hours, one in 12, and one in 15. How long will it be before all three reach Portland?" The experimental second grade "had an almost perfect score." For traditionally schooled ninth graders, 6 out of 29 got the correct answer. The most common wrong answer was 37 hours.

Of course, students taught computational arithmetic make a computation out of the problem. Benezet's curriculum included mathematical reasoning, but not computation. A more difficult problem was this: "There is a wooden pole that is stuck in the mud at the bottom of a pond. There is some water above the mud and part of the pole sticks up into the air. One-half of the pole is in the mud; $2/3$ of the rest is in the water; and one foot is sticking out into the air. Now, how long is the pole?"

Students from traditional sixth-grade classes were unable to compute themselves through a problem that involved two different fractions and one measure of length. His experimental fifth-grader said, "One-half of the pole is in the mud and ½ must be above the mud. If $2/3$ is in the water, then $2/3$ and one foot equals 3 feet, plus the 3 feet in the mud equals 6 feet." It is not surprising that with the time freed up from arithmetic, the experimental classes showed language ability several grade levels above traditional classrooms. Nor is it surprising that all classrooms were soon returned to traditional arithmetic, where they remain today.

Robert I. Lerman and Arnold Packer in *Education Week* April 21, 2010, write: "When the state's chief test-maker was asked why New York tested students' ability to factor a polynomial but not to speak standard English, even though good verbal skills matter far more on the job to far more people. The answer? 'Because we can test factoring but not speaking.'" I wonder how much this answer explains why so much of our math curriculum is never used after graduation.

Lerman and Packer continue:

> Consider Algebra II, the study of logarithms, polynomial functions, and
> quadratic equations. Although many states want to make the course a

requirement for graduating from high school, there appears no need to do so. Northeastern University sociologist Michael J. Handel has found that only 9 percent of people in the workforce ever use this knowledge, and that fewer than 20 percent of managerial, professional, or technical workers report using any Algebra II material. In fact, the National Assessment of Adult Literacy shows that more than 20 percent of adults (and about 50 percent of minority adults) never learn fractions well enough to apply them to common tasks. When we fixate on Algebra II's polynomial functions, command and depth of knowledge are sacrificed for ill-learned, and quickly forgotten, breadth.

I downloaded the new Common Core State Standards for mathematics and English language arts. Here's a favorite of mine from the high school standards: "Know and apply the Remainder Theorem: For a polynomial $p(x)$ and a number a, the remainder on division by x-a is $p(a)$, so $p(a) = 0$ if and only if $(x$-$a)$ is a factor of $p(x)$." I get lost in the grocery store aisles every time I forget this one, or worse, I forget to look both ways before stepping into the street.

An America Diploma Project benchmark for algebra holds that all students should be able to "determine the 126th term of the arithmetic sequence whose third term is 5 and seventh term is 29." Good grief!

"How do you explain school to a higher intelligence?"

—ELLIOT, *E.T.: THE EXTRA-TERRESTRIAL*

William Farish (1759–1837) was a professor of chemistry at the University of Cambridge. He was unusual in that he also taught about the mechanical principles of machinery used in manufacturing industries, inventing isometric projection for the purpose of his lectures. He designed and installed a movable partition wall in his

Cambridge home that moved on pulleys between downstairs and upstairs. He would pull down the partition when he felt cold working late at night.

In 1792 he was just a tutor, and his income was proportional to the number of students tutored. In those days a student's quality was judged not by grades or institution attended, but by what the professor taught and could vouch that the student had learned. Teaching and learning was more of an intimate relationship, and class sizes were necessarily small. Farish was practical, inventive, and modern for his time. He invented the university examination and associated grading system to replace considered opinion of the teacher as evaluation. This allowed immediate expansion of the number of students served and of his income.

Like all human inventions, grades were just hanging around waiting for an inventor, and Farish was the first to bump into them. The fact that he was weird allows us to make some fun of both him and his invention.

From Neil Postman in *Technopoly:* The "idea that a quantitative value should be assigned to human thoughts was a major step towards constructing a mathematical concept of human reality. If a number can be given to the quality of a thought, then a number can be given to the qualities of mercy, love, hate, beauty, creativity, intelligence, even sanity itself." This efficiency has so wiggled its way into our culture that when talking to a student, one might ask, "How are your grades?" as naturally as asking, "How are you?"

The high road, as defined by Andrew Bryk in *Organizing Schools for Improvement*, is "Schools should form in every child the capacity to think and act well in an increasingly complex, pluralistic, democratic society." Jerome Bruner suggested in the *Harvard Educational Review* that school be a place where "students can experience success and failure not as reward and punishment but as information." We hear incessantly, and generally believe, the unintended negative consequences of grading, or more generally, scoring. Intrinsically it invites gaming at every level: by student, teacher, school, district, state, and nation. The fundamental defect is applying a quantitative

measure on a qualitative "capacity to think and act well." A tape measure will never assess the beauty of a Michelangelo statue.

Yet, (a) the test numbers are not going to go away, replaced solely by Her Majesty's Inspectorate of Education's observation and narrative or some equivalent qualitative assessment, and (b) the numbers *do* measure something; there are too many correlations and patterns. For example, it is clear that poverty and race make a big difference in a child's potential for success in a society dominated by these numbers. The real question is what do these numbers tell us about how and why school experiences do or do not build that capacity in students to think and act well in the various environments they might experience, including that of school itself?

We are entering a period where there is going to be much attention paid to testing, both to the design of the tests and to the interpretation. It is my hope that this attention will uncover what these numbers *really* mean and how to use them to improve our public and private decisions. It will be a political decision about what to do with the new tests and their numbers; one can hope that good information will lead not to simply getting better numbers, but to getting better schools.

Jose Ferreira admits in his article "Standardized Realities" for *Education Week*, "I began taking standardized tests for fun. I would take them in the morning with a cup of coffee, the way other people do crosswords. I found a hidden structure to standardized tests that makes them quite easy. And hilarious. I was obsessive, taking every GMAT, LSAT, SAT, and GRE that had ever been published. I took an MCAT once just for laughs. I don't know any science, but I did well enough that I could have gotten into medical school."

I was happy to read this, for I, too, have an easy time with standardized tests. Young August, on the other hand, struggles. I talked with him at length as he described how he "attacked" a multiple-choice question. He would argue with each proposed answer, demanding that it prove itself true and under what conditions. Almost always there were several answers that could be true under certain conditions; confused and frustrated, he would pick one for no good reason except to be done with it.

As his teacher, I would describe August as argumentative. He would greet new information with a "Yes, but ... " which I wouldn't respond to until finally he would declare not "I got it!" but "You win."

I explained to him my technique, which is to just "listen" to each answer, listening for the sounds of deceit. Easy enough, as we have all been lied to plenty of times before and learned to get on with it. The capacity for detailed argumentation is indeed a life skill, one treasured by the lawyer class, but so is the capacity for recognizing simple deceits.

"I tried not to let myself question the test's usefulness while going through it because it would just make me angry and, no matter what, I would still have to do it. The test was just another hoop I had to jump through in order to advance. Viewed in the most positive light, jumping through hoops is a useful life skill," another student once explained to me.

Being at ease with standardized tests is indeed a life skill, related more to one's ability to make sensible decisions and to avoid the obvious potholes of life than to one's knowledge of subject matter.

"The skills needed to do well on these tests at best
reflect a shallow kind of learning and at worst
indicate only a better ability to take tests."

—George Wood

"Education ... has produced a vast population able to
read but unable to distinguish what is worth reading."

—George Macaulay Trevelyan

M ight it be that classrooms in poverty pockets have characteristics that reflect the character of poverty itself?

Alfie Kohn recently elaborated in *Education Week* on Martin Haberman's description of the "pedagogy of poverty" from an article for *Kappan* written in 1991. Kohn pointed out that the testing driving No Child Left Behind is making it worse. "Haberman described a tightly controlled routine in which teachers dispense, and then test students on, factual information; assign seatwork; and punish noncompliance." He quotes Natalie Hopkinson: "In the name of reform ... education—for those 'failing' urban kids, anyway—is about learning the rules and following directions. Not critical thinking. Not creativity. It's about how to correctly eliminate three out of four bubbles."

Kohn notes that "those who demand that we 'close the achievement gap' generally focus only on results, which in practice refers only to test scores. High-quality instruction is defined as whatever raises those scores." He quotes Haberman: "The overly directive mind-numbing ... anti-intellectual acts that pass for teaching" in urban schools "not only remain the coin of the realm but have become the gold standard."

Kohn adds:

> Not only is the teaching scripted, with students required to answer fact-based questions on command, but a system of almost militaristic behavior control is common, with public humiliation for noncompliance and an array of rewards for obedience that calls to mind the token economy programs developed in prisons and psychiatric hospitals.

> Deborah Meier ... points out that the very idea of "school" has radically different meanings for middle-class kids, who are "expected to have opinions," and poor kids, who are expected to do what they're told. Schools for the well-off are about inquiry and choices; schools for the poor are about drills and compliance. The two types of institutions "barely have any connection with each other," she says.

Kohn then quotes Linda Darling-Hammond: "The most counterproductive [teaching] approaches [are] enforced most rigidly in the schools serving the most disadvantaged students." Kohn adds this zinger: "The rich get richer, while the poor get worksheets." This pedagogy of poverty is not just what teachers do and students expect, but what parents and the community involved assume teaching to be in their schools. It is likely a central fixture in the phenomenon of poverty.

The article Haberman wrote in 1991 describes the relationships in the classroom as being responsible for schools' part in the emergence of poverty. He writes:

> Students in urban schools overwhelmingly do accept the pedagogy of poverty, and they do work at it! Indeed, any teacher who believes that he or she can take on an urban teaching assignment and ignore the pedagogy of poverty will be quickly crushed by the students themselves. Examples abound of inexperienced teachers who seek to involve students in genuine learning activities and are met with apathy or bedlam, while older hands who announce, "Take out your dictionaries and start to copy the words that begin with *h*" are rewarded with compliance or silence ...
>
> But below this facade of control is another, more powerful level on which students actually control, manage, and shape the behavior of their teachers. Students reward teachers by complying. They punish by resisting. In this way students mislead teachers into believing that some things "work" while others do not. By this dynamic, urban children and youth effectively negate the values promoted in their teachers' teacher education and undermine the nonauthoritarian predispositions that led teachers to enter the field. And yet, most teachers are not particularly sensitive to being manipulated by students. They believe they are in control and are responding to "student needs," when, in fact, they are more like hostages responding to students' overt or tacit threat of noncompliance and, ultimately, disruption.

It cannot be emphasized enough that, in the real world, urban teachers are never defined as incompetent because their "deprived," "disadvantaged," "abused," "low income" students are not learning. Instead, urban teachers are castigated because they cannot elicit compliance. Once schools made teacher competence synonymous with student control, it was inevitable that students would sense who was really in charge.

The students' stake in maintaining the pedagogy of poverty is of the strongest possible kind: it absolves them of responsibility for learning and puts the burden on the teachers, who must be accountable for making them learn.

Kohn and Haberman seem to be scolding the schools for not stopping the pedagogy of poverty, as if fixing schools would fix society. I know community organizers who say, "Look, getting them off the streets and into classrooms, learning to obey and work hard is a significant first step; don't deny us that first step. And by the way, as long as you who rule our society make social/economic advancement equal to test scores, you have to acknowledge that our test scores did indeed get better. Don't be so arrogant as to tell us what we 'ought' to do; leave us alone to heal ourselves in our own ways."

I say no, no, we can't just leave you alone. We need to tell each other some stories and start a conversation based upon them.

"Schools in the ghetto become schools of the ghetto."

—CHARLES M. PAYNE

"For some, not learning *was a strategy that made it possible for them to function on the margins of society instead of falling into madness or total despair."*

—HERBERT KOHL

Richard Elmore, in his book *School Reform from the Inside Out*, emphasizes a principle of reciprocity for performance-based accountability systems. "For each unit of performance I demand of you, I have an equal and reciprocal responsibility to provide you with a unit of capacity to produce that performance, if you do not already have that capacity." Well, of course, don't ask the chef to make a soufflé without giving her a soufflé pan … "Asking people to do the impossible without helping them to master the skills necessary to do it is a recipe for political resistance and ultimate failure." It's just not fair, either.

Not that long ago school accountability was all about *inputs*: teacher degrees, licensure, professional development hours, seat time for students, textbook choices, and so on. I don't remember when performance-based, or outcome-based, assessment began, but I first heard of it from Tony Alvarado. Tony had been superintendent of District 4 schools in NYC and was the one who, in 1974, invited Deborah Meier, a kindergarten teacher fresh from Chicago, to found Central Park East Elementary School. He said something like, "If we get the outcomes we want, what does it matter what the inputs are?" That makes sense too, but does it pass the fairness test, the principle of reciprocity?

Outcome-based accountability became assessment-based when schools turned to standardized tests to measure student achievement, and the Bush No Child Left Behind Act made that the way American public education did its business. One of the very few good outcomes of NCLB has been a wealth of student test data. The data clearly show that student achievement is not affected by the traditional measures of inputs mentioned above. We can also say that measuring student achievement and the achievement gap between haves and have-nots did not inform us about how to raise the scores or reduce the gap. Assorted schools were identified where scores were low and were highly correlated with measures of poverty. But every student, parent, or teacher who ever walked the halls of these schools already knew they were abominable.

It is not that assessing inputs is not appropriate, it's that the traditional measures mentioned above proved themselves less than useful. It's as deep and subtle as the biblical moral injunction "As ye sow, so shall ye reap." If you want a cheese soufflé you need eggs, white sauce, cheese, and that soufflé pan—and yes, some serious instruction and practice. The principle of reciprocity requires that we be as accountable for inputs as for outcomes. Let's list some criteria for accountability:

- Interferes minimally with the learning processes
- Is both quantitative and qualitative
- Is both objective and subjective
- Must not be culturally biased, where poverty is recognized as a culture
- Must be regarded as understandable and fair by those being held accountable

We can aptly compare how we practice medicine in this country to how we educate our children. Yes, there is much quantitative data, blood pressure, white cell count, etc., but in the end the key measure is "How do you feel? Is there anything that is bothering you?" John Goodlad stated that "healthy nations have healthy schools, it's not the other way around." OK, true, and then true too that healthy schools have healthy classrooms. If the definition of health is "possessing soundness and vigor, freedom from disease or ailment," then what are the characteristics of a healthy classroom? Would it be easier to identify healthy classrooms than all this balancing of inputs and outcomes? I think the answer may be yes. For one thing, while inputs look at what the teacher brings to the classroom and outcomes look at what students take out, looking at the whole classroom integrates teacher and students into one element of study. My own experience as a teacher is that it is an almost instantaneous read whether or not a classroom is "healthy." In any open discussion, disease will announce itself.

The question of healthy classrooms and healthy schools, then, is a question of having open discussions, and an open discussion is both an input and an output.

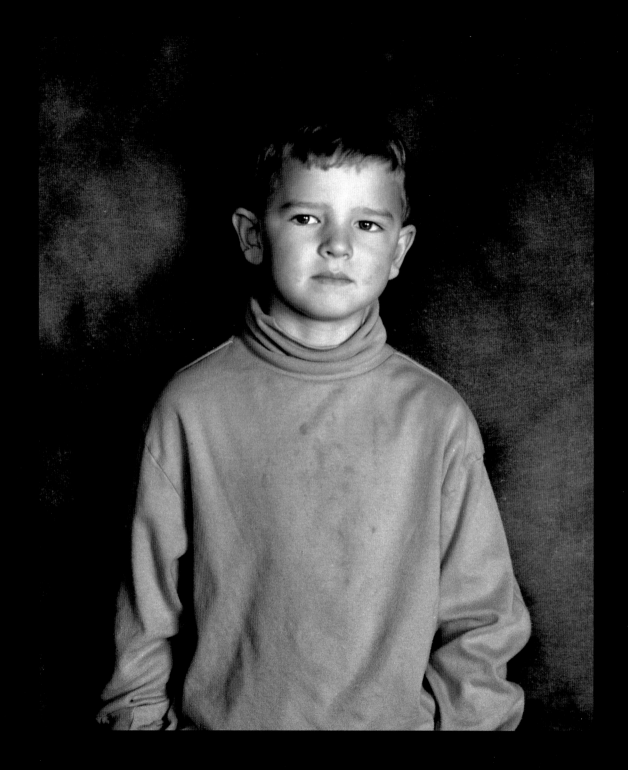

"Who needs the most practice talking in school?
Who gets the most?"

—Bill Hull

My first year of teaching, as much as I wanted to be the world's greatest teacher, I wanted even more to be just like all the rest of the teachers in the school, to just be accepted as one of the guys, to belong. It's a skill that I've worked on along the way to becoming an adult, how to be a chameleon, at least on the outside.

One of the myths we sustain about education is that teaching is a profession. No, I say teaching is a craft—craftsmen have guilds or unions, professionals have their accrediting associations. One way the profession myth is propagated is by subjecting teachers to "professional development," emphasis on the first word. If we teachers buy in at all, it's that "if we are indeed a profession, then it's the worst paid profession of all." I actually prefer, for myself, to use the word "craft"; like a cabinetmaker, teachers are able to sand down the rough edges of an adolescent.

Soon enough came my first inservice experience (our terminology for "professional development"). It's a Friday afternoon, no classes, the kids go home, we go to the meeting room. The principal introduces our trainer, who works for some educational consulting firm; the title of the seminar is "The Fives Es of Excellence" or something like that. The reasonably nice-looking woman starts talking and writing on the whiteboard, but I'm watching my colleagues. I want to behave just like them, no sticking out. They shuffle their chairs around and talk to each other pretty loudly. So I do too, and this goes on for the whole hour, at the end of which we give a weak round of applause and are dismissed.

Now I like my classes, but it is demanding work, and an afternoon off is welcome. It seems like we all liked it, behaving exactly as we always hoped our students wouldn't. Our attitude was "Oh, Miss Goody Two-Shoes sits in front and asks questions, but we never liked her anyway." We repeated this behavior at all inservices thereafter. In another life I found myself presenting an inservice to high school science teachers. My subject was the quark model of the elementary particles, and I choose to present it at the sophomore honors level in liberal arts, a level I was familiar with from my past as both a high school teacher and a university professor of physics. The teachers wiggled their chairs around, opened the chips bought for their snack break, and talked to each other pretty loudly. OK, fair's fair.

On an education blog I read:

> Adminstrators in Mei Flower's district, having decided that teachers needed just half a day of classroom preparation before the onslaught of classes, planned a half-day inservice for the afternoon. The program included such standards as the Pledge of Allegiance (this went well. We knew all the words.) and an address by the local union president, plus "special" fare like a slideshow from the previous year (I already lived through last year, thanks, let's move on.) and local kids singing a medley of Broadway show tunes. By that time everyone was more than ready to leave. But instead, they were treated to a "professional speaker"—a lawyer with enunciation problems … All we can say is that there's a reason for the similarities in the terms "inservice" and "serving time."[5]

And in the same blog Renee Moore writes: "The afternoon of the third day, they brought in a VERY expensive, so-called motivational speaker who made us all stand and sing the old Kenny Rogers tune, *You Picked a Fine Time to Leave Me Lucille* (all the verses)."

The system counts these inservices as continuing education units, and they inch one up the pay scale.

---

5. http://blogs.edweek.org/teachers/blogboard/archives/2006/08/inservice_day.html.

*"Don't ever confuse what teachers (or any people)
say they think and feel with what they think
and feel in the quiet of their nights."*

—Seymour Sarason

Teaching: a white-collar middle-class profession, right, isn't that the stereotype? Sure, they know their subject matter—in second grade its runny noses—but outside of their specialty area they're boring, preoccupied with school and school politics. Politically they're a little left, but don't know enough about the real world to explain why. What do they say, "Those who can, do; those who can't, teach"? People say, "Of course we need them; kids gotta get educated, and we need to get to work. It doesn't quite add up that white-collar middle-class professionals have a teachers' union; unions are supposed to be a blue-collar thing ... "

Governor John Kasich (R) of Ohio has said, "If they want to strike, they should be fired. They've got good jobs, they've got high pay, they get good benefits, a great retirement. What are they striking for?" The governor speaks for many, if not for teachers themselves. Here are some background facts:

Colleges of education enroll primarily from the lower academic 25 percent of students.

Thirty-three percent of new teachers leave within three years, 50 percent within five years. Richard Ingersoll, in his 2001 report *Teacher Turnover, Teacher Shortages, and the Organization of Schools*, analyzes organizations through studying the amount and causes of employee turnover. This is a remarkably high turnover, and Ingersoll notes, "High levels of employee turnover are both cause and effect of dysfunction and low performance in organizations." His report is an analysis of the reason teachers leave so quickly: "In particular, low salaries, inadequate support from the school administration, student discipline problems, and limited faculty input into school decision-making." Other reasons for dissatisfaction Ingersoll charts include lack of student motivation, class sizes too large, inadequate time to prepare, unsafe environment, poor opportunity for professional advancement, lack of community support, interference in teaching, lack of professional competence of colleagues, and intrusions on teaching time.

We hear the plain talk from those in charge that the goal is for every high school graduate to be career or college ready. This is accounted for not by whether they go to or complete college or what jobs they take, but by standardized test scores. We hear that the way to this goal is a good teacher in front of every class. The plan seems to be roughly this: First we'll learn how to measure a teacher's goodness, then we'll learn how to identify those with the potential to become good teachers, then learn how to train them. And then, damn the unions, we'll fire all the bad teachers and replace them with our brand-new good ones.

My personal experience with good teachers is that there are many dimensions to the goodness, and it goes well beyond the capacity to "deliver instruction." To be done well, the job of a classroom teacher demands all the skills of any other skilled profession. In other words, if schools want good teachers they will have to compete against many other careers for the kind of good people required. Indeed, teaching needs to be a good career in order to attract the folks who can be good teachers. Ingersoll gave you the reasons teachers left. Here are some quotes I personally heard from some who stayed:

- It's like trying to dance in a girdle.
- Every school has its internal assassins.
- The faculty is divided and arguing; this makes me want to just shut the door and stay isolated.
- I don't feel safe in school until I close the door to my room.
- There are too many missions, too many different forces, too much diversity in the kids, too much diversity in the parents.
- I give to the kids, I give to the parents; there's nothing left for me to give to me.

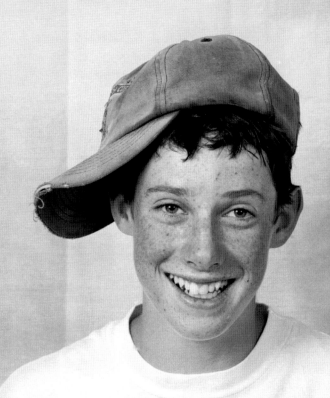

- If you do something great it's called rocking the boat.
- We are driven by the school calendar: the cleaning schedule, bus routes, lunch schedule, etc.
- Neither teachers nor students are trusted to make important decisions about their lives in school.
- The community, the nation as a whole, doesn't support education.

Ingersoll concludes that:

> Popular education initiatives, such as teacher recruitment programs, will not solve the staffing problems of such schools if they do not also address the organizational sources of low teacher retention …

> The data show that the solution to staffing problems does not primarily lie in increasing an insufficient supply, but rather in decreasing excess demand. In short, this analysis suggests that recruiting more teachers will not solve staffing inadequacies if large numbers of such teachers then leave.

> Current policies will not only not solve school staffing problems, but they will also divert attention from the primary underlying problem—the manner in which schools are managed and teachers are treated.

It is inherently difficult for a large public institution based upon compulsory attendance, i.e., involuntary participation by its consumers, to avoid oppression upon its lower levels. Teachers lie just above students at the bottom of the heap.

"The reward of teaching is knowing that
your life makes a difference."

—William Ayers

W ashington, D.C., in late June is as good a place as any to brood about the predicament of our humanity.

It is hot and the streets are available to all; this is a democracy. There are blacks, there are whites and browns, those who speak English and those who speak many other languages. There are more Italian restaurants along this section of Connecticut Avenue these days, but not more speakers of Italian. We find an English restaurant, two Greek restaurants, no French, yet a Nepalese restaurant. Everybody has decent clothes and shoes.

There are joggers, dog walkers, sidewalk sweepers, sightseers, shoppers, homeless, panhandlers, and the crazies: the mumblers, the shouters, these strange people seeming to be not a bit of this world, yet here and now interacting with me, strange small social acts along this street, in this manner that I cannot quite fathom and I find disturbing. A young man sits on the corner, he looks like a jogger, hair combed, stopped for a rest. He salutes as I pass and shouts, "Watch! Watch!" I hear him for the next half block; I know he is still talking to me. Something new has come into my being.

The brain develops, in size and in complexity of nerve structure, from an embryo, and all embryos look so much alike! How is it we become so different from such sameness? Of course, inside that embryo is the union of DNA from two parents, but that too has a sameness, even when looked at under the microscope. There is a sameness along Connecticut Avenue, too. Skin color and hairdos vary considerably, but almost everyone has two arms, ten fingers, two legs, ten toes, a face with two eyes, etc. Hat sizes vary a scant $3/8$ inch, indicating a nearly universal brain mass inside. Yes, there's a sameness along Connecticut Avenue, but not an equalness. "Watch!" he yelled, and it was very loud, very demanding.

The brain develops in an evolutionary sense, meaning that it grows, makes connections and disconnections, according to some "survival of the fittest" criterion. Connections are made inside the developing brain that differentiate between subtle sounds, subtle visual effects, subtle distinctions felt by all the senses. The mind, we say, grows epigenetically, making new connections based on the connections made previously; the code in the DNA is not there to say which connections are to be made, only that they are to be made in this epigenetic fashion. Given the way in which a given brain develops, it strives to evolve itself in such a fashion as to make its owner an effective contributor to the survivability of itself and of the species.

We, our brains, interact with our sensory experiences and "learn" from them. No two brains either begin identically or experience the same history of sensory inputs, thus we, our brains, learn to be different, to be unique. "Watch!" he yelled, and I quickened my pace and realized that I am what I not yet am.

> *"Like a child, without a story I*
> *cannot explain myself."*
>
> —Vivian Gussin Paley

It is important to note the distinction between "epistemology," a set of beliefs about knowing, and "ontology," a set of beliefs about what exists or what is real. Constructivist epistemologies posit that individuals construct their own realities, and no two realities will be exactly the same. Each of us has a uniquely constructed version of reality that we carry around with us in our day-to-day experience as human beings. Two people looking at something together never actually see the same thing in the same way. Everybody's reality is a historically developed "state of the mind" resulting from individual and differentiated experiences.

> *"Is 4 the 4 for everybody?*
> *Are all sevens equal?*
> *When the convict ponders light is it the same*
> *light that shines on you?"*
>
> —Pablo Neruda

This is consistent with the view that the brain is the major organ of the mind and is composed of a unique set of neurons and a unique set of synapses, both sets determined by inheritance and experience. The current state of the mind is simply the result of building and destroying neurons, the building, strengthening, weakening, and disappearance of synapses. No two brains are identical. There is no one true ontology.

Social-constructivist learning theory is now conventional wisdom about how people, including schoolchildren, learn. "To learn" means to construct a new state of the mind by adding new experiences to the former construction, thus creating a new construction. When we hyphenate the word "social" into the theory of learning, we are simply acknowledging that we are very social beings and most of our important experiences are social interactions among us beings.

Constructivism demands that knowledge is not absolute, that it depends on whose mind we are talking about; it is relative to the person holding the knowledge. This does not mean that Denver may or may not be the capital of Colorado. For one mind it is "I had to memorize state capitals in fifth grade, and this is what I remember for Colorado," for another it is "I looked at a map and saw that Denver was pictured as a star, and I interpret that to mean that it is a capital," and for another, "I have driven by and seen the golden dome of the capitol building," to another …

Just as in constructing anything, there are degrees of quality of the construction, from well-constructed and solid to poorly constructed and sloppy. The degree is associated with workmanship or craftsmanship; how much care and work went into placing the pieces just so? In good construction the fits are tight, the finish durable, and there is overarching functionality that is suitable for and invites further construction. Schools and their classrooms are supposed to be the venue of much serious mental construction. Teachers design and consult on eatch student's construction. We want the design to be big enough and complex enough to hold the whole child and the life that he or she will lead. The construction itself, the figurative sticks and nails, are a collaboration between teacher and student. The teacher is an observer, a consultant, critic, and fan of each student's work, and always supporting higher levels of craftsmanship.

So teaching is helping each child build his own knowledge according to his existing structures and their future needs. Didn't I mention before that the life of a teacher is complicated? And then there's the social part: how does a teacher organize the social structures such that each child's construction project interacts with all of the other construction projects? Social constructivism requires good workmanship here, too, if the structures that are the whole classroom together are to be durable and robust.

When I feel like I am teaching well, I am as confused as my students; we are together on that.

"Intelligence" derives from the Latin verb *intellegere*, "to understand, to realize, to discern." Not very sharply defined by the Romans, it was a loose bundle of characteristics of mental capacity. The age of scientific rationality is unable to leave a word like that loosely defined and not measurable. It took fifty-two researchers to report in *Mainstream Science on Intelligence* (1994) that intelligence is "a very general mental capability that, among other things, involves the ability to reason, plan, solve problems, think abstractly, comprehend complex ideas, learn quickly and learn from experience. It is not merely book learning, a narrow academic skill, or test-taking smarts. Rather, it reflects a broader and deeper capability for comprehending our surroundings— 'catching on,' 'making sense' of things, or 'figuring out' what to do." This is still a pretty loosely defined bundle of characteristics, but I have just enough intelligence to get it. I suppose it's another one of those things, like pornography, that is difficult to describe but we know it when we see it.

Intelligence, then, is largely the ability to get along pretty well no matter what the situation, even new or unusual situations. In "Where Is Intelligence?" David Perkins describes it as "knowing your way around" the contexts of your life. Getting along in unusual situations and knowing your way around provide a definition that works for all developmental stages. Let us look at the years normally spent in school, the time of formal education that we defined as "The act or process of imparting or acquiring general knowledge, developing the power of reasoning and judgment, and generally of preparing oneself or others for a mature life that has meaning." Clearly there are many similarities and overlaps between intelligence and education. I think that it is true that "figuring out what to do" to succeed in school requires intelligence. I think it is also true that having intelligence provides no particular motive for taking school seriously as preparation for a mature life that has meaning, and many intelligent kids don't take it seriously.

There is an interesting phenomenon around intelligence. In spite of the fact that it is so difficult to define in words, some paper-and-pencil exercises—tests, really—have been developed that produce scores, i.e., numbers typically translated as IQ, that correlate with many other numbers that capture elements of this commonsense abstraction we call intelligence.

Often what we measure has no direct relationship to other things that the measurement correlates to. For example, the mercury in my living room barometer has nothing physically connecting it or interacting with the weather system, yet the height of the mercury column correlates with many properties of the weather because it is proportional to the barometric pressure of the atmosphere. We learn to take correlations seriously, even if we don't see cause-and-effect relationships.

Different IQ tests correlate among themselves. IQ correlates positively with SAT scores, school grades, other achievement tests, job performance, incomes, and social status. Individuals with low IQs are more likely to be divorced, have a child out of wedlock, be incarcerated, and need long-term welfare support.

"The having of wonderful ideas is what I consider
the essence of intellectual development."

—Eleanor Duckworth

We, children or adults, describe someone as intelligent, smart, quick, savvy, or knowing their way around. It is interesting that I never hear any argument about such a judgment when assorted folks with assorted knowledge and experience agree and nod their heads. It's like sitting out in the sun in August and someone says, "Hot, ain't it?" and everybody agrees without having to add degrees or modifiers. Same thing with intelligence: "She's smart, eh?," and we all nod in agreement.

Teachers are particularly attuned to noting this particular characteristic. We need to almost read the students' minds in order to teach, and that reading includes some understanding of their highly individualized smartnesses.

"Intelligence" is the word that captures most of what we mean: "The capacity for learning, reasoning, understanding, and similar forms of mental activity; aptitude in grasping truths, relationships, facts, meanings, etc." The word comes from Latin, "to choose between." The ancients wrestled with just what it is, and today's thinkers, with advanced statistical methods, have devised many experiments that provide quantitative data that show some common categories among different people and reproducible numerical results for individuals. Whenever intellectuals try to categorize such abstractions as thoughts and mental activities, there will be strong disagreements. What is perhaps a commonsense commonality is that there is a general intelligence, a very general mental capability that, among other things, involves the ability to reason, to plan, solve problems, think abstractly, comprehend complex ideas, learn quickly, and learn from experience, a broader and deeper capacity for comprehending our surroundings, "catching on," "making sense" of things, or "figuring out" what to do. This is a nontechnical conventional wisdom description of what is called "general intelligence," or "g intelligence," and it is what the better IQ tests measure to some approximation. Then there are *specific* intelligences, like in mastering chess, algebra, PhotoShop, the arts, and so on.

It has always struck me that the mental capacity required to do well on standardized tests is simply that of specific intelligence, with the converse being that what standardized tests measure is primarily general intelligence. There is a correlation of .82 between

IQ scores and SAT scores. The best predictor of how a student will do on any high school standardized test is how she did on her first test in third grade. More suggestive is this: Researchers at the University of Minnesota measured attachment patterns of children at forty-two months and could predict within 77 percent accuracy who would graduate from high school. Throwing in IQ and test achievement data did not allow the researchers to improve on that prediction's accuracy. Now school standardized tests also test for the specific knowledge and skills that have been taught. The high correlation simply suggests the obvious, that those with higher general intelligence, and/or those with high attachment patterns, absorb more facts and skills from the classroom experience.

So, we don't know exactly what IQ tests measure, nor do we know exactly what standardized tests measure, but they correlate and both are reliable indicators of intelligence, whatever that might be.

The question before education policymakers is "Should we use students' test scores to evaluate their teachers?" If test scores are just a reflection of the students' general intelligence, then many would answer, "No, the teacher cannot be held responsible for that over which they have no control." That is a simple answer if we assume that a teacher has no power over student intelligence. When I worked in an alternative, progressive primary school where student responsibility held higher stakes than test scores, I always told the teachers, "If you give the students activities that cause them to reason, to plan, solve problems, think abstractly, comprehend complex ideas, learn quickly and learn from experience, and to gain a broader and deeper capacity for comprehending their surroundings, it follows that they will do fine on any test." And I believe that. If the teacher gives them activities that balance challenge with their individual skills, they get an intellectual "workout" that also achieves the pleasure that Csikszentmihalyi calls "flow." They will learn the techniques and pleasures of using their minds well.

Good teachers will have good student test scores, and it's not the other way around, that good test scores mean good teaching. There's just no easy answer to evaluating teachers, and if good teaching is important to us, we must be willing to look at difficult answers.

REFERENCES

Achieve, Inc., The Education Trust, and The Thomas B. Fordham Foundation. *Ready or Not: Creating a High School Diploma that Counts*. Washington, DC: American Diploma Project, 2004.

Apple, Michael W., and James A. Beane, eds. *Democratic Schools: Lessons in Powerful Education*. Portsmouth, NH: Heinemann, 2007.

Auguste, Byron, Paul Kihn, and Matt Miller. "Closing the Talent Gap: Attracting and Retaining Top-Third Graduates to Careers in Teaching." McKinsey & Company, Sept. 2010.

Ayers, William. *To Teach: The Journey of a Teacher*. New York: Teachers College Press, 1993.

Baldwin, James. "A Talk to Teachers." *The Saturday Review*, Dec. 21, 1963.

Bobbitt, John Franklin. *What the Schools Teach and Might Teach*. Cleveland, OH: The Survey Committee of the Cleveland Foundation, 1915.

Brady, Marion. "Why Thinking 'Outside the Box' Is Not So Easy (And Why Present Reform Efforts Will Fail)." *Education Week*, Aug. 30, 2006.

Bruner, Jerome. *The Process of Education: Towards a Theory of Instruction*. Cambridge, MA: Harvard University Press, 1960.

Bryk, Andrew. *Organizing Schools for Improvement: Lessons from Chicago*. Chicago: University of Chicago Press, 2010.

Bushaw, William J., and Shane J. Lopez. "A Time for Change: The 42nd Annual Phi Delta Kappa/Gallup Poll of the Public's Attitudes toward the Public Schools." *Phi Delta Kappan* 92, no. 1 (Sept. 2010).

Central Advisory Council for Education. *Children and their Primary Schools* (The Plowden Report). London: HMSO, 1967.

Clemens, Sydney Gurewitz. *The Sun's Not Broken, a Cloud's Just in the Way: On Child-Centered Teaching*. Mt. Rainier, MD: Gryphon House, 1983.

Csikszentmihalyi, Mihaly "Iron Mike." Flow: *The Psychology of Optimal Experience*. New York: Harper & Row, 1990.

Darden, Edwin C. "School Law." *American School Board Journal* 198, no. 5 (May 2011).

Darling-Hammond, Linda. *Evaluating Teacher Effectiveness: How Teacher Performance Assessments Can Measure and Improve Teaching*. Washington, DC: Center for American Progress, 2010.

Dawkins, Richard. The *Selfish Gene*. Oxford: Oxford University Press, 1976.

Dewey, John. *The School and Society*. Chicago: University of Chicago Press, 1899.

Dillard, Annie. *The Living*. New York: HarperCollins, 1992.

Duckworth, Eleanor. *The Having of Wonderful Ideas and Other Essays on Teaching and Learning*. New York: Teachers College Press, 1995.

Elmore, Richard F. "I Used to Think...and Now I Think...: Reflections on the Work of School Reform." *Harvard Education Letter* 26, no. 1 (Jan./Feb. 2010). www.hepg.org/hel/article/434.

Elmore, Richard F. *School Reform from the Inside Out: Policy, Practice, and Performance*. Cambridge, MA: Harvard Education Press, 2004.

Elmore, Richard F. "What Would Happen if We Let Them Go." *Futures of School Reform* blog entry for *Education Week*, May 17, 2011.

Falk, John, and Lynn Dierking. "The 95 Percent Solution." *American Scientist* 98, no. 6 (Nov./Dec. 2010).

Ferreira, Jose. "Standardized Realities." *Education Week* 29, no. 21 (Feb. 10, 2010).

Freire, Paulo, and Ira Shor. *A Pedagogy for Liberation: Dialogues on Transforming Education*. South Hadley, MA: Bergin & Garvey Publishers, 1987.

Gardner, John W. *No Easy Victories*. New York: Harper & Row, 1968.

Gassaway, Bernard. "Teachers." *Teachers College Record*, Feb. 22, 2008.

Goodlad, John I. *Teachers for Our Nation's Schools*. San Francisco: Jossey-Bass, 1990.

Greenberg, Daniel. *Free at Last*. Framingham, MA: Sudbury Valley School Press, 1995.

Greene, Maxine. *Variations on a Blue Guitar: The Lincoln Institute Lectures on Aesthetic Education*. New York: Teachers College Press, 2001.

Haberman, Martin. "Pedagogy of Poverty Versus Good Teaching." *Phi Delta Kappan* 73, no. 4 (Dec. 1991).

Holt, John. *What Do I Do Monday?* New York: Dutton, 1970.

Horton, Myles. "The Community Folk School." In *The Community School*, edited by Samuel Everett. New York: D. Appleton-Century, 1938.

Hutchins, Robert M. *The Conflict in Education in a Democratic Society*. New York: Harper, 1953.

Ingersoll, Richard. "Teacher Turnover, Teacher Shortages, and the Organization of Schools." *American Educational Research Journal* 38, no. 3 (Fall 2001).

Johnston, Michael. *In the Deep Heart's Core*. New York: Grove Press, 2002.

Kennedy, Mary M. "The Mysterious Gap between Reform Ideals and Everyday Teaching." *Inside Teaching: How Classroom Life Undermines Reform*. Cambridge, MA: Harvard University Press, 2005.

Kohl, Herbert. *"I Won't Learn from You" and Other Thoughts on Creative Maladjustment*. New York: New Press, 1994.

Kohn, Alfie. "Poor Teaching for Poor Children…in the Name of Reform." *Education Week*, April 27, 2011. www.alfiekohn.org/teaching/edweek/poor.htm.

Kuntner, Mark, Elizabeth Greenberg, Ying Jin, and Christine Paulsen. *The Health Literacy of America's Adults: Results from the 2003 National Assessment of Adult Literacy (NCES 2006-483)*. Washington, DC: US Dept. of Education, National Center for Education Statistics, 2006.

Lakoff, George. *Moral Politics: What Conservatives Know That Liberals Don't*. Chicago: Chicago University Press, 1996.

Lakoff, George. *The Political Mind: Why You Can't Understand 21st-Century Politics with an 18th-Century Brain*. New York: Viking, 2008.

Lerman, Robert I., and Arnold Packer. "Will We Ever Learn? What's Wrong with the Common-Standards Project." *Education Week*, April 21, 2010.

Madison, James. "The Federalist No. 10." *The Federalist Papers*, Nov. 23, 1787.

Martin, Jane Roland. *The Schoolhome: Rethinking Schools for Changing Families*. Cambridge, MA: Harvard University Press, 1992.

Meier, Debbie. *The Power of Their Ideas: Lessons for America from a Small School in Harlem*. Boston: Beacon Press, 1995.

Morris, Henry. *The Village College: Being a Memorandum on the Provision of Educational and Social Facilities for the Countryside, with Special Reference to Cambridgeshire*. Cambridge, England: Cambridge University Press, 1924.

Mursell, James. *Principles of Democratic Education*, New York: W. W. Norton, 1955.

National Governors Association and the Council of Chief State School Officers. Common Core State Standards. www.corestandards.org.

National Research Council. *Reshaping School Mathematics: A Philosophy and Framework for Curriculum*. Washington, DC: National Academy Press, 1990.

Neruda, Pablo. *The Book of Questions*. Translated by William O'Daly. Port Townsend, WA: Copper Canyon Press, 1991. Originally published as *Libro de las preguntas* (Buenos Aires, Argentina: Losada, 1974).

Offe, Claus, and Ulrich Preuss. "Democratic Institutions and Moral Response." In *Political Theory Today*, edited by David Held. Stanford, CA: Stanford University Press, 1991.

Olson, Kirsten. *Wounded by School: Recapturing the Joy in Learning and Standing Up to Old School Culture*. New York: Teachers College Press, 2009.

Paley, Vivian Gussin. *The Kindness of Children*, Cambridge, MA: Harvard University Press, 1999.

Paley, Vivian Gussin. *You Can't Say You Can't Play*. Cambridge, MA: Harvard University Press, 1992.

Palmer, Parker. *And a Little Child Shall Lead Them*. Philadelphia: Friends Publishing, 1978.

Parham, Janis N., and Stephen P. Gordon. "Moonlighting: A Harsh Reality for Many Teachers." *Phi Delta Kappan* 92, no. 5 (Feb. 2011).

Payne, Charles M. *So Much Reform, So Little Change: The Persistence of Failure in Urban Schools*. Cambridge, MA: Harvard Education Press, 2008.

Perkins, David. "Where Is Intelligence?" *Educational Leadership* 51, no. 8 (May 1994).

Perry, Theresa, Robert Moses, Joan T. Wynne, Ernesto Cortés Jr., and Lisa Delpit. *Quality Education as a Constitutional Right: Creating a Grassroots Movement to Transform Public Schools*. Boston: Beacon Press, 2010.

Postman, Neil. *Technopoly: The Surrender of Culture to Technology*. New York: Knopf, 1992.

Postman, Neil, and Charles Weingartner. *Teaching as a Subversive Activity*. New York: Delacorte Press, 1969.

Progressive Education Association. The Eight-Year Study. 1942.

Ravitch, Diane. *The Death and Life of the Great American School System: How Testing and Choice Are Undermining Education*. New York: Basic Books, 2010.

Rippa, S. Alexander. *Education in a Free Society: An American History*. New York: D. McKay, 1967.

Rothbard, Murray. *For a New Liberty: The Libertarian Manifesto*. New York: Macmillan, 1973.

Shelley Evans-Marshall v. Board of Education of the Tipp City Exempted Village School District, 624 F.3d 332 (6th Cir. 2010).

Shulman, Lee. *The Wisdom of Practice: Essays on Teaching, Learning, and Learning To Teach*. San Francisco: Jossey-Bass, 2004.

Stoelinga, Sara Ray. "Pressuring Teachers to Leave: Honest Talk about How Principals Use Harassing Supervision." *Phi Delta Kappan* 92, no. 4 (Dec. 2010/Jan. 2011).

Trevelyan, George Macaulay. *English Social History: A Survey of Six Centuries, Chaucer to Queen Victoria*. London: Longmans, Green, 1942.

Whitehead, Alfred North. "The Aims of Education." In *The Aims of Education and Other Essays*. New York: Macmillan, 1929.

Wiggins, Grant. "A Diploma Worth Having." *Educational Leadership* 86, no. 6 (March 2011).

Wigginton, Eliot. "A Song of Inmates." *Educational Leadership* 51, no. 4 (Dec. 1993/Jan. 1994).

Willingham, Daniel T. *Why Don't Students Like School? A Cognitive Scientist Answers Questions about How the Mind Works and What it Means for the Classroom*. San Francisco: Jossey-Bass, 2009.

Yazzie-Mintz, Ethan. *Charting the Path from Engagement to Achievement: A Report on the 2009 High School Survey of Student Engagement*. Bloomington, IN: Center for Evaluation and Education Policy, 2010.

SELECTED READINGS

Gardner, Howard. *The Unschooled Mind: How Children Think and How Schools Should Teach.* New York: Basic Books, 2004.

Hawkins, David. *The Informed Vision.* New York: Algora Publishing, 2002.

Vygotsky, Lev S. *Mind in Society: The Development of Higher Psychological Processes.* Cambridge, MA: Harvard University Press, 1978.

Vygotsky, Lev S. *Thought and Language.* Cambridge, MA: MIT Press, 1986.

Wenger, Etienne. *Communities of Practice: Learning, Meaning, and Identity.* Cambridge, England: Cambridge University Press, 1998.